Contributions to Neuropsychological Assessment

Contributions to Neuropsychological Assessment
A Clinical Manual

ARTHUR L. BENTON

Emeritus Professor of Psychology and Neurology,
University of Iowa

KERRY deS. HAMSHER

Assistant Professor of Neurology, University of Wisconsin;
Director of Neuropsychology, Mount Sinai Medical Center, Milwaukee, Wisconsin

NILS R. VARNEY

Assistant Professor of Neurology, University of Iowa;
Staff Psychologist, Veterans Administration Center, Iowa City, Iowa

OTFRIED SPREEN

Professor of Psychology, University of Victoria, British Columbia

New York   Oxford
OXFORD UNIVERSITY PRESS
1983

Library of Congress Cataloging in Publication Data
Main entry under title:

Contributions to neuropsychological assessment.

  Bibliography: p.
  Includes index.
  1. Neuropsychology—Handbooks, manuals, etc.
I. Benton, Arthur Lester, 1909–
[DNLM: 1. Psychological tests. 2. Psychophysiology.
3. Neurophysiology. WM 145 C764]
QP360.C665 1983   152   82-7822
ISBN 0-19-503192-X   AACR2
ISBN 0-19-503193-8 (pbk.)

Printing (last digit): 9 8 7

Printed in the United States of America

To
Maurice Van Allen

Preface

This manual describes some of the neuropsychological tests which my colleagues and I have utilized in clinical and investigative work during the past 20 years. The tests are of a diverse nature. Some, such as Facial Recognition and Judgment of Line Orientation, have a broad area of application. Others, such as Pantomime Recognition and Phoneme Discrimination, are special procedures designed for use with patients in particular diagnostic categories when a specific question arises.

In most instances a test was developed to answer a specific question or meet a specific need. One example is our test of tactile form perception which was constructed to aid in the interpretation of defective tactile naming in aphasic patients. In order to help to decide whether a defective performance was of a strictly linguistic nature or instead might reflect a failure in recognition because of perceptual impairment, it was sometimes felt necessary to evaluate the patient's capacity for tactile recognition of abstract figures through the nonverbal matching-to-sample procedure incorporated in the test. Subsequently the test was found to be useful in a broader context to assess spatial thinking in the somesthetic modality in nonaphasic as well as aphasic patients.

Another example is our test of facial recognition. The original version was devised to probe for evidence of "facial agnosia" in patients with brain disease. However, we and other investigators discovered that performance on this task requiring the discrimination of unfamiliar faces was not significantly related to the clinical complaint which had to do with the identification of the faces of familiar persons. At the same time, we found that a remarkably large number of patients with focal brain disease performed poorly on the test and that it showed promise of being a sensitive indicator of at least certain types of cerebral dysfunction. Consequently, it was revised and standardized for clinical use.

Twelve tests are described in this volume. Specific directions for administration, scoring, and interpretation are given and the clinical application of each test is discussed. As will be seen, many of the tests involve the use of special material such as pictures, blocks, or a videotape.

Over the years many colleagues have collaborated in the development of these tests, among them Henry L. Dee, Mary Fangman, Max L. Fogel, Musetta C. Gordon, Kerry deS. Hamsher, Robert J. Joynt, Harvey S. Levin, Otfried Spreen,

F. Beth Stone, Maurice W. Van Allen, and Nils R. Varney. It is a great pleasure to acknowledge their contributions. I am particularly pleased that Kerry Hamsher, Nils Varney, and Otfried Spreen, whose participation in this program of test development was especially important, agreed to be co-authors of this manual.

The authors are indebted to Dr. Abigail B. Sivan for aid in the preparation of the manual and to Mrs. Jean Hulme who typed the manuscript.

November 1982   A.L.B.

Contents

List of Figures

List of Tables

Contributions to Neuropsychological Assessment

1. Temporal Orientation

BACKGROUND

Assessment of the accuracy of a patient's temporal orientation is included in practically every mental status examination. The reason for its inclusion is obvious. Accurate temporal orientation is an essential component of mental competence and impaired orientation implies the presence of some type of abnormal condition: dementia, confusion, an amnesic syndrome, delusional psychosis, mental deficiency, and even malingering are among the possibilities.

Gross temporal disorientation as reflected, for example, in misstating the year or missing the hour of day by several hours can hardly escape the attention of a clinical examiner. However, he may be at a loss to interpret the significance of minor inaccuracy in orientation, such as misstating the day of the week or month by a day or two, unless he has at hand reliable information about the range of normal variation. In general, neurologists' estimates of what can be regarded as "normal" tend to be rather liberal, i.e., their conception of the range of normal variation is somewhat broader than is indicated by empirical data (cf. Benton, Van Allen & Fogel, 1964; Natelson, Haupt, Fleischer & Grey, 1979).

The brief test described below was designed to meet the need for a standardized procedure based on empirically established norms that would provide a more solid basis for interpreting the performances of patients. It was standardized on two independent samples of normal subjects in Iowa (Benton, Van Allen & Fogel, 1964; Levin & Benton, 1975) and subsequently Natelson, Haupt, Fleischer & Grey (1979) reported normative observations on a sample of subjects in New Jersey. The utility of the test was demonstrated by the finding that it disclosed impaired orientation in 27 patients with brain disease, only 13 of whom had been judged to be temporally disoriented at routine clinical examination (Benton, Van Allen & Fogel, 1964; Levin & Benton, 1975).

DESCRIPTION

The content, administration, and scoring of the test are shown in Table 1-1. As will be seen, five responses are scored—the stated day of week, day of month,

3

TABLE 1-1   Test of Temporal Orientation

Administration

What is today's date? (The patient is required to give month, day, and year.)
What day of the week is it?
What time is it now? (Examiner makes sure that the patient cannot look at a watch or clock.)

Scoring

Day of week: 1 error point for each day removed from the correct day to a maximum of 3 points.
Day of month: 1 error point for each day removed from the correct day to a maximum of 15 points.
Month: 5 error points for each month removed from the correct month with the qualification that, if the stated date is within 15 days of the correct date, no error points are scored for the incorrect month (for example, May 29 for June 2 = 4 error points).
Year: 10 error points for each year removed from the correct year to a maximum of 60 points with the qualification that, if the stated date is within 15 days of the correct date, no error points are scored for the incorrect year (for example, December 26, 1982 for January 2, 1983 = 7 error points).
Time of Day: 1 error point for each 30 minutes removed from the correct time to a maximum of 5 points.

The total number of error points constitutes the patient's obtained score.

---

month, year, and time of day. The examiner should keep in mind that misstating the year or the month is not penalized if the actual date is close to the date of transition from one year or month to the next. The failing responses of an aphasic patient should be interpreted with caution even when his understanding and expression of speech have been judged to be adequate for taking the test.

NORMATIVE OBSERVATIONS

The distributions of the test scores of 434 normal subjects representing the combined samples of the studies by Benton, Van Allen, and Fogel ($n=110$); Levin and Benton ($n=70$); and Natelson, Haupt, Fleischer, and Grey ($n=254$) are shown in Table 1-2. The subjects in the studies of Benton et al. and Levin and Benton were patients using the medical and surgical services of the University of Iowa Hospitals. Those in the study of Natelson et al. were drawn from a variety of sources such as visitors' waiting rooms of hospitals and a shopping mall.

It will be seen that the majority of subjects made perfect scores and that 93% made scores of 0–2 error points. A score of 3 can be classified as borderline since it is exceeded by 93% of the normative group (95% in the Benton studies; 92% in the Natelson study). Scores of more than 3 can be classified as defective since they are exceeded by 95% of the normative group (97% in the Benton studies; 94% in the Natelson study). Analysis of the scores above 3 in the samples of Benton, Van Allen, and Fogel and Levin and Benton disclosed that only two of the 180 subjects in the combined samples made scores of more than 6 and only one made a score of more than 7. On this basis it seems reasonable to consider scores of 4–7 as

TABLE 1-2 Temporal Orientation of Control Subjects:
Distributions of Scores

Error score	Group			
	A[1] (*n*=110)	B[2] (*n*=70)	C[3] (*n*=254)	ABC (*n*=434)
0	67 (61%)	48 (69%)	176 (69%)	291 (67%)
1	33 (30%)	18 (26%)	40 (16%)	91 (21%)
2	4 (4%)	1 (1%)	17 (7%)	22 (5%)
3	3 (3%)	1 (1%)	6 (2%)	10 (2%)
>3	3 (3%)	2 (3%)	15 (6%)	20 (5%)

[1] Benton, Van Allen & Fogel (1964).
[2] Levin & Benton (1975).
[3] Natelson, Haupt, Fleischer & Grey (1979).

moderately defective and scores of 8 or higher (exceeded by 99.4% of normal subjects) as severely defective. This analysis could not be made on the data of the study of Natelson, Haupt, Fleischer, and Grey since all scores above 3 were combined into one category in their report.

Comparing the characteristics of those subjects who made perfect or near-perfect scores (0–1 error point) with those performing below this level, Benton, Van Allen, and Fogel found no differences between groups with respect to age, educational level, Verbal Scale IQ, or sex. Natelson, Haupt, Fleischer, and Grey made the same comparison and, while they found no associations between performance level and age or self-rated health status, they did find that educational level was related to test scores to a modest degree. Specifically, they found that 24% of the subjects with less than 12 years of education made scores above 1 point as compared to only 10% of subjects with 12 or more years of education. The Spearman rank-order correlation coefficient between test score and years of education was .154, which was significant (p <.025) for their large sample of cases. Therefore they suggested that the criteria for evaluating the performance of a patient with less than 12 years of schooling be slightly less strict than for those of a higher educational level.

The most frequent error made both by normal subjects and by patients with brain disease is to miss the day of the month by one or more days. The next most frequent error is to misstate the time of day by more than 30 minutes. In contrast, it is most exceptional for a normal subject to misidentify the year or the month.

PERFORMANCES OF PATIENTS WITH BRAIN DISEASE

The distribution of the scores of the patients in the studies of Benton, Van Allen, and Fogel (1964) and Levin and Benton (1975) as well as a combined distribution

TABLE 1-3 **Temporal Orientation: Distributions of Scores of Patients with Brain Disease**

Error score	Group		
	A[1] (n=60)	B[2] (n=55)	AB (n=115)
0	27 (45%)	24 (44%)	51 (44%)
1	6 (10%)	11 (20%)	17 (15%)
2	12 (20%)	4 (7%)	16 (14%)
3	1 (2%)	3 (5%)	4 (3%)
4	3 (5%)	1 (2%)	4 (3%)
5	3 (5%)	1 (2%)	4 (3%)
6	—	1 (2%)	1 (1%)
7	1 (2%)	—	1 (1%)
8	—	2 (4%)	2 (2%)
9	1 (2%)	—	1 (1%)
10	—	2 (4%)	2 (2%)
11	1 (2%)	—	1 (1%)
12	1 (2%)	—	1 (1%)
> 12	4 (7%)	6 (11%)	10 (9%)

[1] Benton, Van Allen & Fogel (1964).
[2] Levin & Benton (1975).

from the two studies are shown in Table 1-3. None of these patients were aphasic. Not surprisingly, the two distributions are fairly similar; although the two studies were done 10 years apart, they dealt with patients from the same population in the same clinical facility. As will be seen, 27 patients (24%) performed defectively, 10 (9%) of these at a moderately defective level and 17 (15%) at a severely defective level. It will be further noted that the category of "severe defect" encompasses a very wide range of scores and perhaps should be subdivided. Most of the patients with scores above 12 were completely disoriented while those scoring in the 8–12 range showed some degree of preserved orientation, even if it was far from precise.

Among these nonaphasic patients, those with bilateral disease (n=23) showed the highest frequency of defective orientation (57%). In contrast, the proportions of patients with left-hemisphere lesions (n=41) or right-hemisphere lesions (n=51) who performed defectively were much smaller (17% in the left-hemisphere group and 14% in the right-hemisphere group).

There is undoubtedly a significant association of at least moderate degree between temporal disorientation and the presence of general mental impairment. In the study of Benton, Van Allen, and Fogel, 8 (57%) of the 14 patients who performed defectively were judged to have severe general mental impairment. On the other hand, only 13 (28%) of the 46 patients who performed adequately on the temporal orientation test also were judged to have severe general mental impairment. Thus while temporal disorientation is often evident within the setting of a general dementia, it can occur without dementia and, conversely, a demented patient may show adequate temporal orientation.

The temporal orientation questions were given to 15 aphasic patients with left-hemisphere disease who were judged to be testable (Levin & Benton, 1975). Five (33%) performed defectively. Although the examiner felt that these failing performances reflected a true impairment in temporal orientation, the possibility that aphasic misnaming may have been responsible for some incorrect answers could not be excluded. It is perhaps the case that adequate performance by an aphasic patient is more informative than his failure on the test.

Joslyn and Hutzell (1979) utilized the test in a comparative study of temporal orientation in brain-damaged and psychiatric patients in a Veterans Administration neuropsychiatric hospital. Their samples consisted of patients in the following categories: (1) schizophrenics tested shortly after admission; (2) brain-damaged patients tested shortly after admission; (3) alcoholics tested shortly after admission; (4) long-term hospitalized schizophrenics; (5) long-term hospitalized brain-diseased patients. The "admission" groups were not necessarily first admissions; some patients had been hospitalized previously. The fact that the brain-diseased and alcoholic patients were receiving care at a neuropsychiatric rather than a general medical-surgical hospital indicates that behavioral incompetence or disorder was a prominent feature of the clinical picture.

The findings are shown in Table 1-4. As will be seen, both groups of patients with brain disease showed a very high frequency of impaired temporal orientation, far higher than the nonpsychotic neurological patients in the Benton studies. As a group, the admission patients were more impaired than the long-term patients, perhaps because they were more acutely disturbed. In contrast, both groups of schizophrenic patients included relatively few cases with impaired orientation. However, it must be noted that a substantial number of long-term patients, both brain-diseased and schizophrenic, were excluded from the study because they were not cooperative. In any case, it seemed clear that hospitalized schizophrenic patients are less likely to show impaired temporal orientation than even nonpsychotic patients with brain disease. Finally, it will be noted that the alcoholic patients, all of whom had been judged not to have an "organic brain syndrome," performed at a normal level.

REFERENCES

Benton A. L., Van Allen M. W. & Fogel M. L. (1964) Temporal orientation in cerebral disease. *J. Nerv. Ment. Dis. 139*, 110–119.

Levin H. S. & Benton A. L. (1975) Temporal orientation in patients with brain disease. *Appl. Neurophy. 38*, 56–60.

Joslyn D. & Hutzell R. R. (1979) Temporal disorientation in schizophrenia and brain-damaged patients. *Am. J. Psychiat. 136*, 1220–1222.

Natelson B. H., Haupt E. J., Fleischer E. J. & Grey L. (1979) Temporal orientation and education: a direct relationship in normal people. *Arch. Neurol. 36*: 444–446.

TABLE 1-4　Temporal Orientation: Scores of Brain-Damaged, Schizophrenic, and Alcoholic Patients*

Error score	Admission Groups		Long-term Groups		
	Brain-damaged (n=14)	Schizophrenic (n=45)	Alcoholic (n=15)	Brain-damaged (n=18)	Schizophrenic (n=22)
0	2	33	13	8	15
1	2	4	1	1	3
2	2	4	0	1	2
3	0	0	1	1	0
4–6	1	2	0	1	0
7–10	2	2	0	1	1
11–50	2	0	0	1	0
>50	3	0	0	4	1

*Adapted from Joslyn and Hutzell (1979).

TABLE 1-5 Temporal Orientation Record Form

Name _____ No. _____ Date _____

Age _____ Sex _____ Education _____ Handedness _____ Examiner _____

Error Points	Patient's Answer	Correct Answer	Error Score
Month: 5 for each month up to a maximum of 30. Full credit if within 15 days of correct date.	_____	_____	_____
Day of month: 1 for each day up to a maximum of 15.	_____	_____	_____
Year: 10 for each year up to a maximum of 60. Full credit if within 15 days of correct date.	_____	_____	_____
Day of week: 1 for each day up to a maximum of 3.	_____	_____	_____
Time of day: 1 for each 30 min. from correct time up to a maximum of 5.	_____	_____	_____
		Total Error Score	_____

Norms

Error Score	Classification
0–2	Normal
3	Borderline
4–7	Moderately Defective
8+	Severely Defective

Observations on cooperation, understanding, and linguistic competence:

2. Right–Left Orientation

BACKGROUND

The inability of some patients with brain disease to discriminate between the right and left sides of the body was first described in the late 19th century. The defect was usually interpreted as reflecting impairment in spatial thinking (Badal, 1888), in orientation toward one's own body (Pick, 1908), or in the body schema (Gerstmann, 1930). However, Head (1926) regarded right–left disorientation as a form of defective symbolic thinking, a conclusion derived from his observation that many aphasic patients were unable to identify lateral parts on their own body or that of the confronting examiner.

Both types of interpretation have proved to be valid in the sense that both spatial and symbolic determinants enter into almost all right–left discrimination performances (Benton, 1959, 1968; Poeck & Orgass, 1967; Sauguet, Benton & Hécaen, 1971). Table 2-1 lists some aspects of "right–left orientation" in terms of operationally defined components or levels. The list is not at all complete. As will be seen, it does not take account of various other performances that have been studied.

Five components of right–left orientation are identified in Table 2-1. The "own body" components stand in a definite hierarchical relationship to each other. The ability to perform at level "A" (identification of single lateral parts of one's own body) is prerequisite to success on the other "own body" performances. Next in order of difficulty is level "B", the execution of double *uncrossed* commands. The patient (or young child) who cannot execute this type of command correctly will also be unable to execute double *crossed* commands. However, the converse does not hold true. Many patients (and young children) who cannot execute double crossed commands can execute double uncrossed commands.

Correct identification of the lateral body parts of a confronting person (level "D") requires a rotation of 180 degrees in orientation and successful performance implies appreciation of the relativistic nature of the right–left concept. Symbolic and conceptual factors play a greater role here than in the "own body" performances. It is generally the case that patients who have difficulty in localizing

TABLE 2-1   Components of Right–Left Orientation

Orientation toward one's own body

The subject is instructed to:
- A. Point to single lateral body parts on his own body (e.g., his left ear);
- B. Execute double uncrossed commands (e.g., touch his left ear with his left hand);
- C. Execute double crossed commands (e.g., touch his left ear with his right hand.

Orientation toward a confronting person

With the object of orientation being either the confronting examiner or a front-view representation of a person, the subject is instructed to:
- D. Point to single lateral body parts.

Combined orientation toward one's own body and a confronting person

The subject is instructed to:
- E. Place either his left or his right hand on a specified lateral body part of the confronting person (e.g., his right hand on the left ear of the confronting person).

---

on their own body also fail to identify the lateral body parts of the confronting examiner. But occasional exceptions to the rule are observed, i.e., failure on "own body" performances, particularly in the execution of double crossed commands, with successful identification of right and left on the body of the confronting person. Mastery of the "D" level of performance is a prerequisite for successful execution of "E" level commands which requires the combined operation of both the "own body" and "other person" systems of orientation.

Diverse procedures have been used to assess right–left orientation. The patient may be asked to name lateral body parts indicated by the examiner on his own or the examiner's body. He may be required to imitate double crossed or crossed movements of the examiner. Both of these procedures were included by Head (1926) in his "Hand, Eye, and Ear" test battery. The patient may be asked to identify representations of the right or left hand in different postures (Thurstone, 1938; Kao & Li, 1939). Or the patient may be asked to point to lateral body parts on verbal command, as illustrated in Table 2-1. Our own test utilizes the last procedure.

DESCRIPTION

This 20-item test is an abbreviated version of longer schedules employed in earlier research (Benton, 1959; Benton & Kemble, 1960). As noted, it requires the patient to point to lateral body parts on verbal command, the reason for adopting this procedure being that it makes no demands on naming ability. The demands on motor skill are minimal and most hemiparetic patients are able to execute the commands with the affected arm. Modified versions of the test have been

TABLE 2-2   Right–Left Orientation Test, Form A

1. Show me your <u>left</u> hand.
2. Show me your <u>right</u> eye.
3. Show me your <u>left</u> ear.
4. Show me your <u>right</u> hand.

5. Touch your <u>left</u> ear with your <u>left</u> hand.
6. Touch your <u>right</u> eye with your <u>left</u> hand.
7. Touch your <u>right</u> knee with your <u>right</u> hand.
8. Touch your <u>left</u> eye with your <u>left</u> hand.
9. Touch your <u>right</u> ear with your <u>left</u> hand.
10. Touch your <u>left</u> knee with your <u>right</u> hand.
11. Touch your <u>right</u> ear with your <u>right</u> hand.
12. Touch your <u>left</u> eye with your <u>right</u> hand.

*13. Point to my <u>right</u> eye.
14. Point to my <u>left</u> leg.
15. Point to my <u>left</u> ear.
16. Point to my <u>right</u> hand.

17. Put your <u>right</u> hand on my <u>left</u> ear.
18. Put your <u>left</u> hand on my <u>left</u> eye.
19. Put your <u>left</u> hand on my <u>right</u> shoulder.
20. Put your <u>right</u> hand on my <u>right</u> eye.

*A front-view representation of a person may be presented if this is judged to be desirable. The representation should not be less than 15 inches in height and 6 inches in width.

developed for use with patients with a dense hemiplegia who cannot execute commands involving the affected hand. However, these modified versions have not been standardized. Administration time is 5 minutes.

   The items of Form A of the test are shown in Table 2-2. It will be seen that the five components of right–left orientation listed in Table 2-1 are assessed. Form B is a "mirror image" version of Form A in which the commands are reversed (i.e., show me your *right* hand, your *left* eye, etc.). The record sheets for Forms A and B and the modified versions for hemiplegic patients are shown in Tables 2-6, 2-7, 2-8, and 2-9.

ADMINISTRATION, RECORDING, AND SCORING

Utter the commands slowly and distinctly, placing stress on the adjectives "right" and "left" in order to direct the patient's attention to this aspect of his response. If the patient does not respond to a command, it should be repeated. Slowness in responding and failure to respond until a command is repeated should be noted.

   The patient's actual response should be recorded since different types of error can be made, e.g., in responding to the second command, he may point to his left eye or to his right ear. One point is credited for each correct response, including any corrections of an initially incorrect response. No credit is given for partially correct responses.

Systematic Reversal Examination of any sizable group of children is likely to disclose a few who show a systematic reversal in response to instructions, e.g., they will consistently show the right hand when asked to show the left, place the left hand on the right eye when asked to place the right hand on the left eye, etc. (Cénac & Hécaen, 1943; Benton, 1958). The consistency of their reversed responses implies that they can discriminate between the right and left sides of the body but have attached the wrong verbal label to each side. For the most part the phenomenon is seen in young school children but occasionally an aphasic patient will show systematic reversal.

Since it seemed reasonable to differentiate between subjects who show a trend toward systematic reversal and those who show defects in the basic discrimination between right and left, as evidenced by inconsistency in response, a special scoring system is applied to the performances of subjects who make a large number of reversed responses. After the performance has been scored by conventional criteria, a second scoring system, in which reversed responses are counted as correct and conventionally correct responses are scored as failures, is applied and a "reversal" score is obtained. The degree to which the "reversal" score is higher than the conventional score is a measure of the strength of the tendency toward systematic reversal.

Some normal adults, particularly ambidexters and women, state that they lack an intuitive sense of the difference between the right and left sides of the body and hence experience difficulty in making rapid discriminations (Benton, 1959; Harris & Gitterman, 1978; Wolf, 1973). They have to deliberate about the distinction and may rely on visual cues or incipient movements to make an identification. Consequently, their responses on a right—left orientation test may be slow and hesitant. Since our test is untimed, the scores do not reflect any slowness in response that may be associated with such uncertainty or hesitation.

NORMATIVE OBSERVATIONS

The test (Form A or Form B) was given to 234 subjects (126 men, 108 women) within the age range of 16—64 years who were either healthy persons or patients without a history or current evidence of brain disease. The mean test scores of subsamples based on age, sex, and educational level are shown in Table 2-3. As will be seen, there are no noteworthy differences in the mean scores, all of which are quite high. Practically all the errors that were made consisted of misidentifications of a lateral body part of the confronting examiner. "Own body" errors were very rare; no subject made more than one error of this type. It will be noted that the standard deviations in two of the female subgroups are rather high; this reflected the occurrence of scores of 12—13 in two cases in each subgroup. No subject showed systematic reversal in responsiveness.

TABLE 2-3   Right–Left Orientation: Mean Scores

		Age, men		Age, women	
Education		<50 yrs.	50+ yrs.	<50 yrs.	50+ yrs.
12+ yrs.	Mean	19.6	19.7	19.3	19.9
	SD	1.4	.8	2.3	.3
	n	37	6	24	9
<12 yrs.	Mean	19.3	19.4	19.4	18.9
	SD	1.3	1.1	1.1	2.2
	n	47	36	51	24

The distribution of the scores in the normative sample is shown in Table 2-4. The majority of subjects made perfect scores and 96% of the group made scores in the 17–20 point range. Thus a total score of less than 17 can be classified as defective. No subject made more than one error on the 12 "own body" items of the test and the commission of more than one error on these items can also be considered to be a deviant performance.

A number of performance patterns can be defined on the basis of the normative observations:

  A. *Normal.* Total score of 17–20, not more than one error on the 12 "own body" items.
  B. *Generalized defect.* Total score of less than 17, more than one error on the 12 "own body" items.
  C. *"Confronting person" defect.* Total score of less than 17, not more than one error on the 12 "own body" items.
  D. *Specific "own body" defect.* More than one error on the 12 "own body" items, not more than two errors on the eight "confronting person" items.
  E. *Systematic reversal.* Total score of 17–20 when performance is scored in reverse fashion, not more than one error on the 12 "own body" items.

TABLE 2-4   Right–Left Orientation: Distribution of Scores of Control Subjects

	Score									
	20	19	18	17	16	15	14	13	12	<12
n	168	35	14	8	2	1	–	3	3	–

TABLE 2-5   Right–Left Orientation: Performance Patterns in Patients with Brain Disease

Pattern*	Diagnostic category			
	Bilateral (*n*=34)	Right (*n*=20)	Left nonaphasic (*n*=20)	Left aphasic (*n*=20)
A. Normal	12 (35%)	13 (65%)	16 (80%)	5 (25%)
B. Generalized defect	13 (38%)	–	2 (10%)	6 (30%)
C. "Confronting person" defect	9 (27%)	7 (35%)	2 (10%)	8 (40%)
D. Specific "own body" defect	–	–	–	1 (5%)
E. Systematic reversal	–	–	–	–

*See text for definition of patterns.

PERFORMANCE OF PATIENTS WITH BRAIN DISEASE

Table 2-5 presents the test results for 94 righthanded patients in four diagnostic categories: (1) nonaphasic patients with right hemisphere lesions (*n*=20); (2) nonaphasic patients with left hemisphere lesions (*n*=20); (3) aphasic patients with left hemisphere lesions (*n*=20); (4) patients with bilateral disease (*n*=34). All patients were able to use both hands in executing the commands and were given Form A or Form B of the test. The findings are presented in terms of the performance patterns defined on the basis of the normative data.

There was only one instance of a specific "own body" defect (i.e., Performance Pattern D—more than one error on the 12 "own body" items without at least three errors on the 8 "confronting person" items). The patient was a 65-year-old woman with a porencephalic cyst in the left posterior parietal area who showed a mild fluent aphasia with marked alexia and agraphia. She made 3 errors on the 4 double crossed commands, 2 errors on the 4 double uncrossed commands, no errors on the 4 single confrontation commands, and 2 errors on the 4 "combined orientation" commands. No patient showed systematic reversal (Performance Pattern E). Scoring in reverse fashion yielded a higher score than did the conventional scoring in some patients, but in no case was the reversal score as high as 17.

As Table 2-5 shows, generalized defect (Performance Pattern B) and "confronting person" defect (Performance Pattern C) were shown by a high proportion of patients with bilateral disease (most of whom were at least moderately demented) and those with aphasic disorder. In contrast, generalized deficit was shown by only a very small proportion of nonaphasic patients with unilateral disease. The patients with right hemisphere lesions showed only "confronting person" failures. Failure of any type was uncommon in the group of nonaphasic patients with left hemisphere disease.

COMMENTS

The findings in our sample are in excellent agreement with the earlier observations of Sauguet, Benton, and Hécaen (1971) who compared the right–left orientation performances of aphasic patients with left hemisphere disease, nonaphasic patients with left hemisphere disease, and nonaphasic patients with right hemisphere lesions. The "own body" test was failed by 29% of the aphasic patients but by only 3–4% of the nonaphasic patients. The "confronting person" test was failed by 43% of the aphasics, by 4% of the nonaphasic patients with left hemisphere lesions, and by 16% of the nonaphasic patients with right hemisphere lesions.

It is quite clear that right–left disorientation with respect to one's own body is uncommon in patients who are not aphasic or demented. Given the tendency for patients with right hemisphere lesions to show lateral neglect, it was somewhat surprising to find that in our sample none of the patients in that diagnostic category failed to point to their left body parts. The answer is perhaps to be found in the fact that only patients who had recovered from the acute stage of their illness and were able to undergo one hour or more of neuropsychological testing were selected for study. Thus, although it may be possible to elicit evidence of lateral neglect by cancellation or visual search tests, the patients are not likely to show the gross neglect seen in the acute poststroke stage.

However, as Table 2-5 indicates, many nonaphasic patients with right hemisphere lesions do misidentify the lateral body parts of a confronting person. The question can be raised as to whether the defect is due to a failure to reverse orientation without any lateral bias or to a specific failure to point to the confronting person's right body parts, i.e., body parts in the patient's left visual field. To assess this possibility, the records of 10 patients with right hemisphere lesions who had made 3 or more errors on the 8 confronting person items were examined to determine whether or not a bias toward misidentifying the right parts on the confronting person was present. The results were negative. All the performances were characterized either by a failure to reverse orientation with respect to both the right and left parts of the confronting person or by using the left hand instead of the right (or vice versa) in executing the four "combined orientation" commands.

The close association of right–left disorientation with both aphasia and dementia has raised the question of whether or not the deficit should be considered to have a specific neuropsychological significance. There has been much debate on the question (Benton, 1959, 1977; Frederiks, 1969; Gerstmann, 1957; Orgass & Poeck, 1968; Poeck, 1975; Poeck & Orgass, 1967). A consensus has yet to be reached.

TABLE 2-6   Right-Left Orientation, Form A

Name _____ No. _____ Date _____

Age _____ Sex _____ Education _____ Handedness _____ Examiner _____

Own Body	**Response**	**Score**

1. Show me your left hand.   _____   + – R
2. Show me your right eye.   _____   + – R
3. Show me your left ear.   _____   + – R
4. Show me your right hand.   _____   + – R
5. Touch your left ear with your left hand.   _____   + – R
6. Touch your right eye with your left hand.   _____   + – R
7. Touch your right knee with your right hand.   _____   + – R
8. Touch your left eye with your left hand.   _____   + – R
9. Touch your right ear with your left hand.   _____   + – R
10. Touch your left knee with your right hand.   _____   + – R
11. Touch your right ear with your right hand.   _____   + – R
12. Touch your left eye with your right hand.   _____   + – R

SUM _____

Examiner's Body

13. Point to my right eye.   _____   + – R
14. Point to my left leg.   _____   + – R
15. Point to my left ear.   _____   + – R
16. Point to my right hand.   _____   + – R
17. Put your right hand on my left ear.   _____   + – R
18. Put your left hand on my left eye.   _____   + – R
19. Put your left hand on my right shoulder.   _____   + – R
20. Put your right hand on my right eye.   _____   + – R

SUM _____

Performance Pattern

A. Normal   _____
B. Generalized Defect   _____
C. "Confronting Person" Defect   _____
D. Specific "Own Body" Defect   _____
E. Systematic Reversal   _____

Total Score _____
Reversal Score _____
Comments: _____
_____
_____

TABLE 2-7   Right–Left Orientation, Form B

Name _____ No. _____ Date _____

Age _____ Sex _____ Education _____ Handedness _____ Examiner _____

Own Body	**Response**	**Score**

1. Show me your right hand. _____   + – R
2. Show me your left eye. _____   + – R
3. Show me your right ear. _____   + – R
4. Show me your left hand. _____   + – R
5. Touch your right ear with your right hand. _____   + – R
6. Touch your left eye with your right hand. _____   + – R
7. Touch your left knee with your left hand. _____   + – R
8. Touch your right eye with your right hand. _____   + – R
9. Touch your left ear with your right hand. _____   + – R
10. Touch your right knee with your left hand. _____   + – R
11. Touch your left ear with your left hand. _____   + – R
12. Touch your right eye with your left hand. _____   + – R

SUM _____

Examiner's Body

13. Point to my left eye. _____   + – R
14. Point to my right leg. _____   + – R
15. Point to my right ear. _____   + – R
16. Point to my left hand. _____   + – R
17. Put your left hand on my right ear. _____   + – R
18. Put your right hand on my right eye. _____   + – R
19. Put your right hand on my left shoulder. _____   + – R
20. Put your left hand on my left eye. _____   + – R

SUM _____

Performance Pattern

A. Normal	_____	Total Score _____
B. Generalized Defect	_____	Reversal Score _____
C. "Confronting Person" Defect	_____	Comments: _____
D. Specific "Own Body" Defect	_____	_____
E. Systematic Reversal	_____	_____

TABLE 2-8   Right–Left Orientation, Form R*

Name _____ No. _____ Date _____

Age _____ Sex _____ Education _____ Handedness _____ Examiner _____

Own Body	**Response**	**Score**
1. Show me your left hand.	_____	+ – R
2. Show me your right eye.	_____	+ – R
3. Show me your left ear.	_____	+ – R
4. Show me your right hand.	_____	+ – R
5. Touch your left ear with your left hand.	_____	+ – R
6. Touch your right eye with your left hand.	_____	+ – R
7. Touch your right knee with your left hand.	_____	+ – R
8. Touch your left eye with your left hand.	_____	+ – R
9. Touch your right ear with your left hand.	_____	+ – R
10. Touch your left knee with your left hand.	_____	+ – R
11. Touch your right ear with your left hand.	_____	+ – R
12. Touch your left eye with your left hand.	_____	+ – R
	SUM _____	

Examiner's Body		
13. Point to my right eye.	_____	+ – R
14. Point to my left leg.	_____	+ – R
15. Point to my left ear.	_____	+ – R
16. Point to my right hand.	_____	+ – R
17. Put your left hand on my left ear.	_____	+ – R
18. Put your left hand on my left eye.	_____	+ – R
19. Put your left hand on my right shoulder.	_____	+ – R
20. Put your left hand on my right eye.	_____	+ – R
	SUM _____	

Performance Pattern

A. Normal _____   Total Score _____

B. Generalized Defect _____   Reversal Score _____

C. "Confronting Person" Defect _____   Comments: _____

D. Specific "Own Body" Defect _____   _____

*For use with patients who cannot execute commands with the right hand.

TABLE 2-9   Right–Left Orientation, Form L*

Name _____ No. _____ Date _____

Age _____ Sex _____ Education _____ Handedness _____ Examiner _____

Own Body	Response	Score
1. Show me your right hand.	_____	+ − R
2. Show me your left ear.	_____	+ − R
3. Show me your right ear.	_____	+ − R
4. Show me your left hand.	_____	+ − R
5. Touch your right ear with your right hand.	_____	+ − R
6. Touch your left eye with your right hand.	_____	+ − R
7. Touch your left knee with your right hand.	_____	+ − R
8. Touch your right eye with your right hand.	_____	+ − R
9. Touch your left ear with your right hand.	_____	+ − R
10. Touch your right knee with your right hand.	_____	+ − R
11. Touch your left eye with your right hand.	_____	+ − R
12. Touch your right eye with your right hand.	_____	+ − R
	SUM _____	

Examiner's Body

	Response	Score
13. Point to my left eye.	_____	+ − R
14. Point to my right leg.	_____	+ − R
15. Point to my right ear.	_____	+ − R
16. Point to my left hand.	_____	+ − R
17. Put your right hand on my right ear.	_____	+ − R
18. Put your right hand on my right eye.	_____	+ − R
19. Put your right hand on my left shoulder.	_____	+ − R
20. Put your right hand on my left eye.	_____	+ − R
	SUM _____	

Performance Pattern

A. Normal _____   Total Score _____

B. Generalized Defect _____   Comments: _____

C. "Confronting Person" Defect _____   _____

D. Specific "Own Body" Defect _____   _____

E. Systematic Reversal _____   _____

*For use with patients who cannot execute commands with the left hand.

REFERENCES

Badal J. (1888) Contribution à l'étude des cécités psychiques: alexie, agraphie, hémianopsie inférieure, trouble du sens de l'espace. *Arch. d'Ophtalmol. 8*: 97-117.

Benton A. L. (1958) Significance of systematic reversal in right-left discrimination. *Acta Psychiat. Neurol. Scand. 33*: 129-137

Benton A. L. (1959) *Right-left Discrimination and Finger Localization: Development and Pathology.* New York: Hoeber-Harper.

Benton A. L. (1968) Right-left discrimination. *Ped. Clin. North America 15*: 747-758.

Benton A. L. (1977) Reflections on the Gerstmann syndrome. *Brain and Language 4*: 45-62.

Benton A. L. & Kemble J. (1960) Right-left orientation and reading disability. *Psychiat. Neurol. (Basel) 139*: 49-60.

Cénac M. & Hécaen H. (1943) Inversion systématique dans la désignation droite-gauche chez certains enfants. *Ann. Médico-Psychol. 101*: 415-419.

Frederiks J. A. M. (1969) Disorders of the body schema. In *Handbook of Clinical Neurology*, Vol. 4, P. J. Vinken & G. W. Bruyn (eds). Amsterdam: North-Holland.

Gerstmann J. (1930) Zur Symptomatologie der Hirnläsionen im Uebergangsgebiet der unteren Parietal- und mittleren Occipitalwindung. *Nervenarzt 3*: 691-695.

Gerstmann J. (1957) Some notes on the Gerstmann syndrome. *Neurology 7*: 866-869.

Harris L. J. & Gitterman S. R. (1978) University professors' self-descriptions of left-right confusability: sex and handedness differences. *Percept. Motor Skills 47*: 819-823.

Head H. (1926) *Studies in Neurology.* London: Oxford University Press.

Kao C. C. & Li M. Y. (1939) Tests of finger orientation: methods for testing right-left differentiation and finger-identification. In *Neuropsychiatry in China*, R. S. Lyman (ed.). Peking: Henri Vetch.

Orgass B., & Poeck K. (1968) Rechts-Links-Störung oder Aphasie? Eine experimentelle Untersuchung zur diagnostischen Gültigkeit der Rechts-Links-Prüfung. *Deutsche. Zeit. Nervenhlk. 194*: 261-279.

Pick A. (1908) Ueber Störungen der Orientierung am eigenen Körper. *Neurol. Centralblatt 34*: 257-264.

Poeck K. (1975) Neuropsychologische Symptome ohne eigenständige Bedeutung. *Aktuelle Neurol. 2*: 199-208.

Poeck K. & Orgass B. (1967) Ueber Störungen der Rechts-Links Orientierung. *Nervenarzt 38*: 285-291.

Sauguet J., Benton A. L. & Hécaen H. (1971) Disturbances of the body schema in relation to language impairment and hemispheric locus of lesion. *J. Neurol. Neurosurg. Psychiat. 34*: 496–501.

Thurstone L. L. (1938) *Primary Mental Abilities.* Chicago: University Chicago Press.

Wolf S. M. (1973) Difficulties in right-left discrimination in a normal population. *Arch. Neurol. 29*: 128–129.

3. Serial Digit Learning

BACKGROUND

Serial digit learning (or "digit supraspan") was first proposed as a clinical method for assessing short-term memory by Zangwill (1943) who reported that some brain-injured patients had an unremarkable digit span (i.e., six or seven digits) but could not learn to repeat an eight- or nine-digit series after repeated trials. He therefore recommended that a digit learning task be used instead of the digit span test for the assessment of short-term memory in patients with known or suspected brain disease. He further contended that rote learning tasks were generally more successful than "immediate memory" tasks, such as digit span, in discriminating between organic and functional disorders of memory.

Drachman and Arbit (1966) compared digit span and the learning of a lengthy series of digits in small groups of patients with known or presumed hippocampal dysfunction and in normal subjects. They found that there was no significant difference between groups in digit span. performance but there was a large and highly significant difference between these groups in the performance of the learning task. These results were amplified in a study by Drachman and Hughes (1971) in which they utilized the digit learning procedure to investigate performance differences between older normal subjects (mean age = 62 years; range = 51–69 years) and amnesic patients. They found that the amnesic patients showed gross impairment while the older normal subjects performed un-remarkably on the digit learning task.

The comparative usefulness of a serial digit learning task vis-à-vis the digit span test in identifying brain disease was explored by Schinka (1974). In this study, groups of brain-diseased and control patients in the age range of 20–64 years were given both tasks and results showed that the digit learning test was much superior to the digit span test in discriminating between the two groups. With cutting scores that maximized diagnostic accuracy, the digit learning task correctly classified 76% of the patients while the digit span task achieved only 58% accuracy. While the two groups in Schinka's study were comparable with regard to age and education, statistical analysis identified both of these variables as significantly related to performance. This indicated a need to define appropriate normative values that control for the influence of these variables on performance before applying the task as a measure of short-term memory in the clinical assessment of mental status.

DESCRIPTION

The test consists of the presentation of either eight or nine randomly selected single digits for a varying number of trials up to a maximum of 12. Form SD8 consists of an eight-digit sequence while Form SD9 consists of a nine-digit sequence. Three alternate versions are provided for each form, as detailed below. Selection of the appropriate test form is primarily based on the patient's age and educational level. Each trial is scored according to the criteria described below. The patient's total score on the task can be referred to a table of percentile scores for interpretation. The test takes 5 to 10 minutes to administer, depending on the patient's performance capability.

ADMINISTRATION

As a general rule, SD9 is given to patients under the age of 65 who have 12 or more years of education and SD8 is given to patients who are 65 or older and those under 65 who have less than 12 years of education. However, this is not a strict rule. There are circumstances in which the examiner may decide that SD9 is more appropriate for some patients in the latter categories, i.e., if the vocational history of a patient with a formal educational background of less than 12 years indicates that he is of at least average intellectual endowment, if an older patient is a college graduate, or if the patient has repeated seven digits on the digit span test.

The examiner says to the patient: *"Now I am going to say a number and I want you to repeat it after me. It's a very long number; it has 9 (or 8) digits, so you are not expected to be able to repeat it after you have heard it only once. I will say the number and then you tell me what you can remember; after that I will say the number again and then you will try to repeat it back to me. The best approach is not to try to memorize the whole number all at once. Try to remember the first few numbers and add more numbers on the later trials. You must try to learn this number and you will be given 12 trials to learn it. This may be a hard task and you will have to concentrate very hard. Try not to interrupt the task; if you have any comments we can discuss them after we have finished. Do you understand? Do you have any questions?"*

The instructions may be repeated or elaborated if the patient has any questions or does not seem to understand the task. An example may be given if this is judged to be helpful. If an example is given, use a five-digit number; employing consecutive numbers may be a convenient way to get the idea across, such as 1-3-5-7-9. When the task is understood, the examiner says: *"Fine, here is the number.*

Listen carefully now." (Select one of the three alternate digit sequences from the appropriate test form.) The digits are spoken at the rate of one digit per second. Discontinue testing after two consecutive correct repetitions. Otherwise, proceed through 12 trials. Encouragement may be given during the course of the learning trials in the form of comments such as *"you are doing fine, try again"* or *"you are getting closer"* or *"you almost have it now."* After a correct repetition say *"That is right; let's try it once more."* If on the subsequent trial the response is incorrect, the examiner may say: *"No, now listen again."*

The three alternate series for Form SD9 are:

    (1) 6 - 1 - 3 - 5 - 2 - 8 - 7 - 4 - 9;
    (2) 3 - 9 - 7 - 4 - 8 - 5 - 2 - 6 - 1;
    (3) 8 - 5 - 2 - 9 - 4 - 1 - 7 - 3 - 6.

The three alternate series for Form SD8 are:

    (1) 9 - 1 - 8 - 5 - 2 - 6 - 7 - 4;
    (2) 3 - 6 - 5 - 9 - 2 - 7 - 8 - 4;
    (3) 4 - 7 - 3 - 8 - 2 - 9 - 1 - 6.

The scoring method originally employed was dichotomous. A response on any particular trial was either entirely correct (score = 1) or incorrect (score = 0). However, observations during the course of collecting normative data indicated that the tasks were mastered with great difficulty by some hospital control patients, perhaps owing to mild attentional disturbances. The two most frequent errors were a reversal in the serial order of two adjacent digits (69 for 96) or the substitution of a single digit (9185*1*674 for 9185*2*674). Brain-diseased patients, on the other hand, manifested a different type of difficulty. Their impairment was in the learning and retention of the digits as exhibited by partial responses. They would repeat the first five or six digits correctly but were unable to extend the series with additional learning trials, i.e., on the 12th trial they would still be repeating only the first five or six digits. Therefore a study was carried out using the test records of hospital control patients to determine the effects of variations in scoring methods on the utility of the test.

This study led to the development of a second scoring system that gives two points for perfectly correct responses and one point for "near-correct" responses, i.e., those characterized by only one simple error, namely, one digit is either omitted, added, or substituted, or there is a simple reversal of two adjacent digits. It was anticipated that the revised scoring method would extend the lower limen of measurement and thereby reduce the "floor effect" on the measurement of performance.

RECORDING AND SCORING

Record the patient's response verbatim. Allow spontaneous corrections. If the patient begins a response with the latter digits in the sequence followed by the initial digits, ask the patient to say it again starting with the first number in the sequence and record this as the response.

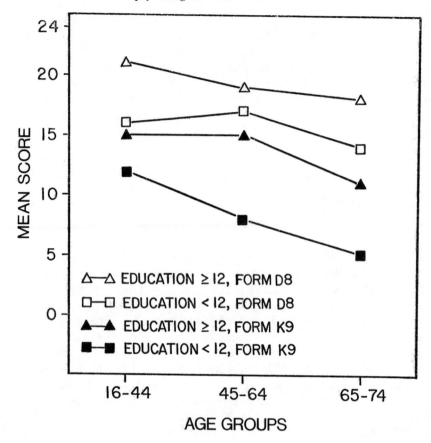

Fig. 3-1 Serial digit learning: Mean performance levels of control patients on Forms D8 and K9. (From K. deS. Hamsher, A. L. Benton & K. Digre (1980). *J. Clin. Neuropsychol.* **2**: 39–50. Reproduced with permission of the publisher)

One point is scored for a "near-correct" response where only one digit is omitted, substituted, or interchanged with an adjacent digit. Two points are credited after a correct repetition. Once the criterion of two consecutive correct repetitions is reached and the task is discontinued, give two points credit for each remaining trial up to and including the 12th trial. The test score is the sum of the points obtained over 12 trials.

Normative Observations   The test was given to a sample of 500 medically hospitalized patients who were without evidence or history of brain disease, psychiatric disorder, or mental defect dating back to childhood (Hamsher, Benton

TABLE 3-1 Serial Digit Learning: Percentile Score Distributions

Form	SD 8				SD 9	
Education	6–11		12–16		6–11	12–16
Age	16–64	65–74	16–64	65–74	16–44	16–64
Scores						
23–24	92	93	82	86	98	97
21–22	84	86	63	72	95	93
19–20	66	74	45	44	84	80
17–18	49	63	27	39	70	64
15–16	40	60	17	33	64	51
13–14	30	49	13	28	57	37
11–12	22	43	9	22	48	31
9–10	19	34	6	17	41	22
7–8	14	29	4	11	36	16
5–6	11	23	3	9	30	10
3–4	8	17	2	6	20	8
1–2	5	11	1	3	14	6
0	2	0	0	0	7	3
n	83	35	142	18	44	178

& Digre, 1980). The age of these patients ranged from 16 to 74 years and educational level ranged from 6 to 16 or more years of schooling. The sample was dichotomized according to educational level; subjects with 6–11 years of education were assigned to the first aggregate, while patients with 12 or more years were assigned to the second aggregate. Within each educational level, subjects were further segregated according to the following age groupings: 16–44 years, 45–64 years, 65–74 years. The same subdivisions were used to obtain normative values for each form of this task.

No differences were found between the performance of men and women on either form of the test. Ethnic background was fairly homogeneous; the sample consisting primarily of Caucasians of European ancestry. At all age levels, education was a significant factor, with subjects of higher educational level performing consistently at a higher level than those with less than 12 years of education. These findings as well as the effects of age are shown in Figure 3-1. As will be seen, there is a consistent decline in performance level in the 65–74 years group as compared to the 45–64 years group. The distribution of performance levels in terms of percentile scores over the range of educational and age levels where one or the other form of this task was considered applicable for clinical use is shown in Table 3-1.

INTERPRETATION OF PERFORMANCE

Interpretation of performance may vary from one population to another depending on base rates and other considerations. The following conventions have been adopted. Scores in the range of the 4th to 7th percentile are considered mildly defective; scores in the range of the 2nd and 3rd percentile are considered moderately defective; scores below the 2nd percentile are considered severely defective. These should be considered general guidelines. Some modification of these interpretations may be required in clinical assessments.

Performance of Brain-Diseased Patients   Hamsher, Benton, and Digre (1980) tested 100 patients with brain disease on the serial digit learning test and at the same time compared their performance on this task vis-à-vis performance on the digit span test. The criterion for subject selection was a final diagnosis of disease involving the cerebral hemispheres which was supported by at least one independent examination, namely, CT scan, radioactive brain scan, angiography, EEG, or a neurosurgeon's operative report. The patients ranged in age from 16 to 73 years, with a mean age of 48 years (SD = 4.5) and their level of education ranged from 6 years to 16 years or more with a mean of 12.6 years (SD = 2.5). None of the patients was clinically aphasic.

The performances of the patients on the serial digit learning and digit span tasks were classified as normal (pass) or defective (fail). The cross-tabulated distribution of performance levels on these two tests is shown in Table 3-2. As will be seen, there is a substantial degree of agreement (69%) between the two performances which is determined for the most part by the large number of patients who passed both tests. In 31% of the cases there was a dissociation in performance. Of these 31 patients, 74% failed digit learning and passed the digit span test, while the converse was seen in 26% of this subgroup. The difference favoring serial digit learning as the test more sensitive to brain disease was determined to be significant by the application of McNemar's test for correlated proportions corrected for continuity ($\chi^2 = 6.23$; $p < 0.02$). The overall sensitivity of the digit span test, i.e., the proportion of brain-diseased patients who were identified as impaired, was 31%. This was significantly less than the proportion who were identified by the digit learning test, which was failed by 46% of the group ($z = 3.08$; $p = 0.002$).

Of the 100 brain-diseased patients, 25 had unilateral left hemispheric lesions, 16 had unilateral right hemispheric lesions, 47 had bilateral hemispheric disease, and, in 12 cases, the extent of the lesion could not be confidently determined. Among patients with unilateral lesions, the frequency of failure on each test was somewhat greater for those with left-sided lesions, but in neither case did this prove to be statistically reliable (Fisher's Exact Probability > 0.10).

Combining both left and right unilateral lesion groups into one, the frequency of defective serial digit learning performances was greater for the patients with bilateral hemisphere disease ($\chi^2 = 5.760$; $p < 0.025$) and, in this subgroup, the

TABLE 3-2 Serial Digit Learning and Digit Span: Performances of Brain-Damaged Patients

Serial digit learning	Digit span	
	Pass	Fail
Pass	46	8
Fail	23	23

TABLE 3-3 Serial Digit Learning and Digit Span: Frequency of Failure in Unilateral Left, Unilateral Right, and Bilateral Hemispheric Disease

Locus	*n*	Frequency of failing performance	
		Digit span	Serial digit learning
Left	25	32%	36%
Right	16	13%	25%
Bilateral	47	36%	60%

From: K. deS. Hamsher, A. L. Benton & K. Digre (1980) *J. Clin. Neuropsychol. 2*: 39–50. Reproduced with permission of the publisher.

serial digit learning task was again more sensitive than the digit span test ($\chi^2 = 4.762$; $p < 0.05$). These results are summarized in Table 3-3.

The results, which demonstrated a superiority of a serial digit learning task over digit span in discriminating brain-diseased from control patients, provide support for Zangwill's original clinical observations and indicate that Schinka's findings, based on selected groups of matched brain-diseased and control patients, may be generalized for clinical application.

REFERENCES

Drachman D. A. & Arbit J. (1966) Memory and the hippocampal complex. II. Is memory a multiple process? *Arch. Neurol. 15*: 52–61.

Drachman D. A. & Hughes J. R. (1971) Memory and the hippocampal complex. III. Aging and temporal EEG abnormalities. *Neurology 21*: 1–4.

Hamsher K, Benton A. L. & Digre K. (1980) Serial digit learning: normative and clinical aspects. *J. Clin. Neuropsychol. 2*: 39–50.

Schinka J. A. (1974) Performances of brain damaged patients on tests of short-term and long-term verbal memory. Ph. D. dissertation, University of Iowa.

Zangwill O. L. (1943) Clinical tests of memory impairment. *Proc. Roy. Soc. Med. 36*: 576–580.

4. Facial Recognition

BACKGROUND

Loss of the ability to recognize the faces of familiar persons was first described as a neuropsychological symptom in 1867 by two Italian ophthalmologists, Antonio Quaglino and Giambattista Borelli. Their patient, a 54-year-old man, was aphasic, showed a paresis of the left arm, and was apparently blind immediately after a stroke. The aphasia and paresis disappeared completely within a few days while the visual defect gradually resolved into a left hemianopia over the course of a month. He was left with three persisting symptoms: an inability to recognize family and friends, impairment in color vision, and defective spatial orientation. The authors' diagnosis was hemorrhage in the right cerebral hemisphere.

Two decades later, when visual agnosia had become a topic of considerable interest to neurologists and ophthalmologists, it was noted that agnosic patients who could not recognize common objects also could not identify the faces of familiar persons and "agnosia for faces" was regarded as part of the syndrome of visual object agnosia. Subsequently, an occasional patient who showed no difficulty in object recognition and whose sole, or at least most prominent, disability appeared to be a loss of the capacity to identify the faces of familiar persons was described. The concept of a specific deficit in facial recognition, designated as "facial agnosia," "agnosia for physiognomies," or "prosopagnosia," arose out of this experience (for reviews of the clinical literature, see Bodamer, 1947; Pallis, 1955; Hécaen & Angelergues, 1962; Rondot & Tzavaras, 1969; Benton & Van Allen, 1972; Lhermitte et al., 1972; Meadows, 1974; Benton, 1980).

It was also found, as Quaglino and Borelli first observed, that patients with facial agnosia generally showed one or more sensory, motor, and behavioral deficits indicative of the presence of right hemisphere disease, such as left hemiplegia, left visual field defect, achromatopsia, spatial disorientation, or visuoconstructive disorder. It was this association with other signs of right hemisphere dysfunction that gave facial agnosia a particular interest and impelled neurologists and neuropsychologists to investigate it in greater detail. However, the deficit occurred too infrequently to permit systematic study. To circumvent this difficulty, clinical investigators devised tests designed to access the accuracy of perception and memory of unfamiliar faces with the aim of determining the anatomic and behavioral correlates of defective performance (cf. Warrington & James, 1967; Benton & Van Allen, 1968; De Renzi, Faglioni & Spinnler, 1968; Tzavaras, Hécaen & Le Bras, 1970). Their initial findings were that impairment in the recognition and memory of unfamiliar faces showed the same association with other signs of right hemisphere disease as did the clinical complaint of facial agnosia and it was assumed that these test procedures, which utilized unfamiliar faces as stimuli, probed the perceptual-mnemonic capacities underlying the recognition of familiar faces.

However, subsequent observations showed that the assumption was untenable. On the one hand, a number of case reports described severely prosopagnosic patients who showed intact ability to recognize unfamiliar faces as assessed by the tests that had been devised (cf. Rondot, Tzavaras & Garcin, 1967; Assal, 1969; Benton & Van Allen, 1972; Tzavaras, Merienne & Masure, 1973). On the other hand, it was observed that most patients whose performances on tests of the recognition of unfamiliar faces were severely defective showed adequate capacity to identify the faces of persons with whom they were familiar. Moreover, while facial agnosia was encountered only rarely, failure in the discrimination of unfamiliar faces was not at all uncommon, particularly in patients with posterior right hemisphere disease. Thus it became evident that impairment in facial recognition could occur in at least two distinctive and essentially independent forms, one represented by a failure to identify the faces of familiar persons (facial agnosia or prosopagnosia) and the other represented by a failure to identify unfamiliar faces which is disclosed by tests developed to assess this capacity.

DESCRIPTION

The purpose of this test is to provide a standardized objective procedure for assessing the capacity to identify and discriminate photographs of unfamiliar human faces. It was first employed in a study of brain-diseased patients in which the relationships between facial recognition and such factors as locus and type of lesion, visual field defect, and aphasia were investigated (Benton & Van Allen, 1968). Subsequently, a Short Form consisting of 27 items was developed, in addition to the original Long Form consisting of 54 response items (Levin, Hamsher & Benton, 1975).

The test consists of three parts:

A. *Matching of identical front-view photographs*. The subject is presented with a single front-view photograph of a face and instructed to identify it (by pointing to it or calling its number) in a display of six front-view photographs appearing below the single photograph. In both versions of the test, three male and three female faces are presented for matching, calling for a total of six responses.

B. *Matching of front-view with three-quarter-view photographs*. The subject is presented with a single front-view photograph of a face and instructed to locate it three times in a display of six three-quarter views, three being of the presented face and three being of other faces. In the Long Form of the test, four male and four female faces are presented for matching, calling for a total of 24 responses. In the Short Form, one male face and three female faces are presented, calling for a total of 12 responses.

C. *Matching of front-view photographs under different lighting conditions.* The subject is presented with a single front-view photograph of a face taken under full lighting conditions and instructed to locate it three times in a display of six front views taken under different lighting conditions; three photographs in the display are of the presented face and three are of other faces. In the Long Form, four male and four female faces are presented for matching, calling for a total of 24 responses. In the Short Form, two male faces and one female face are presented, calling for a total of nine responses.

ADMINISTRATION

The test is assembled in a spiral bound booklet. Each stimulus picture and its corresponding response choices are presented in two facing pages with the single stimulus picture above the six response-choice pictures. If they are able to do so, subjects are encouraged to hold and manipulate the test material to their best visual advantage. Care should be taken to insure that glare is eliminated. Subjects who normally use glasses for close vision should have them available for use.

The test is arranged so that the first 13 stimulus and response display pictures, which comprise the Short Form, are presented first. These are response items 1 through 27 (page numbers 1–13 in the booklet). Following this is a page which identifies the remaining items. Together with the first 27 response items, the latter nine stimulus-response pictures (page numbers 14–22) comprise the 54 response items making up the Long Form.

Procedure: pages 1–6, Short Form and Long Form
Pointing to the single photograph of Item 1, say to the subject: *"You see this young woman? Show me where she is on this picture"* (pointing to the multiple-choice display below). Record correct responses by checking the appropriate item; record errors by circling the appropriate numbers on the right side of the record form. Continue in the same manner for the remaining items through number 6.

Procedure: pages 7–13, Short Form and Long Form
Pointing to the single photograph of page 7, say to the subject: *"You see this young woman? She is shown* three times *on this picture"* (pointing to the multiple-choice display below). *"Show me where she is. Find three pictures of her."* Record the responses of the subject in the same manner as before. Occasionally, after having made two responses, the subject will appear to be at a loss to find the third photograph corresponding to the face represented in the stimulus photograph.

When this occurs he should be told to select the most likely choice among the remaining possibilities. Continue in the same manner for the remaining items of the Short Form. Note that each stimulus picture has its corresponding multiple-choice display on the facing page.

Procedure: pages 14–22, Long Form only
Administration and instructions are the same as above. Note that each stimulus has its corresponding multiple choice display.

Scoring   The Long Form calls for 54 scorable responses. Each correct response is assigned a score of one. A minimum score of 25 may be expected on the basis of chance alone. Hence the effective range of Long Form scores may be considered to be 25–54. For the Short Form the effective range may be considered to be 11–27.

Utilization of the Record Sheet will facilitate recording and scoring. The subject's response can either be checked as being correct or his incorrect response choice(s) can be recorded by circling the appropriate number(s) on the right side of the Record Form (Table 4-1).

If the Short Form is used, record the number of correct responses on the Record Sheet. Then refer to the table for converting to Long Form scores and record that figure. Finally, add the appropriate values to obtain the age- and education-corrected Long Form score.

When the Long Form is used, the total number of correct responses is recorded. The same age and education corrections are applied to both the actual Long Form scores and those which are projected on the basis of the patient's Short Form performance. The interpretations discussed later in this chapter are based on the age- and education-corrected Long Form scores. Age and education corrections are discussed below under "Normative Observations" and they are also given on the Record Sheet.

NORMATIVE OBSERVATIONS

Adults   Normative standards are based on the performances of 286 subjects within the age range of 16–74 years. One sample (196 subjects) consisted of patients from the neurological, neurosurgical, and medical services of the University of Iowa Hospitals, who showed no evidence or history of cerebral disease, who had not been hospitalized for a psychiatric disorder, and whose history did not suggest mental deficiency dating back to childhood. A second sample consisted of 90 normal subjects in the age range of 60–74 years who had volunteered to participate in a study of aging. The findings indicated that age and education, but not sex, were significantly related to performance level.

Analysis of the performances of subjects in the 55–74 age range showed that there was a mean difference of 1.9 points between the performance of those with 12 or more years of education (12+) and those with lesser education (6–11 years). This difference in favor of the better educated group (12+) was statistically

TABLE 4-1   Facial Recognition Test Record Form

Name _____ No. _____ Date _____

Age _____ Sex _____ Education _____ Handedness _____ Examiner _____

Score Conversions				
Short Form	Long Form			
27	54			
26	52			
25	50			
24	49			
23	47			
22	45			
21	43			
20	41			
19	39			
18	37			
17	36			
16	34			
15	32			
14	30			
13	28			
12	27			
11	25			

Short Form (SF)

Page No.	Correct Responses			Errors				
1	(5) ___			1	2	3	4	6
2	(1) ___			2	3	4	5	6
3	(2) ___			1	3	4	5	6
4	(3) ___			1	2	4	5	6
5	(6) ___			1	2	3	4	5
6	(2) ___			1	3	4	5	6
7	(2) ___	(5) ___	(6) ___		1	3	4	
8	(1) ___	(3) ___	(4) ___		2	5	6	
9	(2) ___	(4) ___	(6) ___		1	3	5	
10	(2) ___	(5) ___	(6) ___		1	3	4	
11	(1) ___	(4) ___	(6) ___		2	3	5	
12	(2) ___	(3) ___	(6) ___		1	4	5	
13	(1) ___	(3) ___	(5) ___		2	4	6	

Remaining Items for Long Form (LF)

14	(1) ___	(3) ___	(5) ___		2	4	6
15	(2) ___	(3) ___	(4) ___		1	5	6
16	(2) ___	(4) ___	(5) ___		1	3	6
17	(1) ___	(4) ___	(6) ___		2	3	5
18	(3) ___	(4) ___	(6) ___		1	2	5
19	(2) ___	(3) ___	(4) ___		1	5	6
20	(1) ___	(2) ___	(3) ___		4	5	6
21	(1) ___	(5) ___	(6) ___		2	3	4
22	(2) ___	(4) ___	(5) ___		1	3	6

Score Corrections

	Educ.	
Age	6–11	12+
16–54	0	0
55–64	3	1
65–74	4	2

If Short Form is used, first find Long Form score and then add the correction to it.

SF Score _____ LF Score _____

Correction ___+___

Corrected Long Form Score _____

Normal: 41–54; Borderline: 39–40; Mod. Imp.: 37–38; Severe Imp.: <37;

Observations _____

_____

_____

significant ($p < .01$). However, in the age range of 16–54 years, the difference between educational levels was smaller (0.86 point) and not significant ($p > 0.20$). An education correction of two points was added to the Long Form raw scores of the normal subjects with less than 12 years' education who were 55 years and older.

When educational level was controlled, the mean performance of subjects in the age range of 65–74 years was found to be 1.2 points below the mean performance level of subjects in the age range of 55–64 years. In turn, those in the middle age group (55–64 years) performed 1.6 points below the level of subjects in the age range of 16–54 years. An age correction of one point was added to the Long Form raw scores of subjects between ages 55 and 64 and an age correction of two points was added to the raw scores of subjects between ages 65 and 74.

In summary, normative observations indicated that differences in age and educational level affected test performance to a modest degree. To correct for these influences, Long Form scores were adjusted by adding one point for subjects 55–64 years old who had 12 or more years of education and three points when educational level was below 12 years. In the age range of 65–74 years, two points were added to the Long Form score if education level was 12 or more years and four points were added if education level was less than 12 years. The resulting distribution of corrected Long Form scores is shown in Table 4-2. The men ($n=111$) and women ($n=175$) in our normative sample performed at essentially equal levels, with men obtaining a mean corrected Long Form score of 45.6, and women obtaining a corresponding mean score of 45.1. The mean corrected score for the total sample of 286 subjects was 45.4 (SD = 3.96).

Performances of Children   Samples of children attending the public schools of West Branch, Iowa, ($n=149$) and Washington, Iowa, ($n=117$) were given the facial recognition test and an abbreviated WISC. Age ranged from 6 to 14 years, grade placement from kindergarten to 7th grade, and prorated WISC IQ from 85 to 116. Table 4-3 shows the mean scores at each age level. As indicated, there is a consistent rise in performance level from age 6 to age 14 and the mean score of the 14-year-old children is virtually identical to that of young adults. It will be noted that the increments in performance level between the ages 7 and 9 are small. Assuming that this suggestion of a lag in the growth curve is not due to sampling fluctuation, the finding is consonant with a transition from a "piecemeal" to a "configurational" type of encoding of facial information which has been postulated by Carey and Diamond (1977) to occur at the age of 9 or 10 years.

THE SHORT FORM

As has been mentioned, a short form of the test consisting of 27 items has been developed for use when the time available for examination of a patient is limited. The procedures used to select the items for this Short Form have been described in detail in an earlier publication (Levin, Hamsher & Benton, 1975). Mean

TABLE 4-2   Facial Recognition: Distribution of Long Form Scores in Normal Adults (corrected for age and education, *n*=286)

Corrected Score	Frequency
54	6
53	2
52	5
51	20
50	10
49	26
48	11
47	38
46	23
45	34
44	18
43	33
42	15
41	14
40	7
39	6
38	8
37	6
36	2
35	1
34	1

TABLE 4-3   Facial Recognition: Performances of Children of Normal Intelligence (IQ=85–116)

	Age	*n*	Mean Long Form score
	6	22	33.0
	7	59	37.2
	8	33	37.6
	9	27	38.1
	10	50	40.6
	11	33	41.3
	12	–	–
	13	23	43.0
	14	19	45.1
Total		266	

TABLE 4-4 Facial Recognition: Correlations Between Short Form and Long Form Scores

Group	Production-moment correlation	Probability value
Controls (*n*=151)	.88	*p*<.0001
Brain-damaged (*n*=185	.92	*p*<.0001
Total sample (*n*=336)	.93	*p*<.0001

TABLE 4-5 Facial Recognition: Projected Long Form Scores from Short Form Scores (not corrected for age and education)

Short Form score	Projected Long Form score
27	54
26	52
25	50
24	49
23	47
22	45
21	43
20	41
19	39
18	37
17	36
16	34
15	32
14	30
13	28
12	27
11	25

administration time for the Short Form in the setting of a neurology clinic is 7 minutes with a range of 5–15 minutes.

The obtained correlation coefficients between Short Form and Long Form scores ("part-whole" correlations) for samples of control and brain-diseased patients are presented in Table 4-4. Equivalent Long Form scores for each Short Form score were determined by using the smoothed equipercentile method described by Flanagan (1951). Table 4-5 presents these results. It should be noted that the projected Long Form scores in Table 4-5 are not corrected for age or education.

TABLE 4-6

A. Facial recognition: normative standards. Scores have been corrected for age and education in accordance with Part B.

Corrected score	Percentile rank	Classification
53–54	98+	Very superior
50–52	88–97	Superior
47–49	72–85	High average
43–46	33–59	Average
41–42	16–21	Low average
39–40	8–11	Borderline
37–38	3–6	Defective
<37	1	Severely defective

B. Age and education corrections. If the Short Form is given, convert to a Long Form score (Table 4-5) before adding these corrections.

Age	Education	
	6–11	12+
16–54	0	0
55–64	3	1
65–74	4	2

NORMATIVE STANDARDS

Table 4-6 presents normative standards for adults after age and educational level have been taken into account in determining the corrected Long Form score from either the uncorrected Long Form score or the score projected on the basis of Short Form test performance. Interpretive labels, which may be useful in reporting a patient's performance, are also given. The percentile scores given in Table 4-6 refer to cumulative percentiles. Thus a corrected score of 39, which has a percentile rank of 8, indicates that 8% of control patients scored at or below this level of performance, or, conversely, that this score was surpassed by 92% of controls. Corrected Long Form scores of 39–40 (8th to 11th percentiles) are classified as borderline and may be interpreted as raising the question of an acquired impairment in facial discrimination ability. Corrected scores below 39 are classified as defective, i.e., as indicating an impairment in facial discrimination.

PERFORMANCES OF PATIENTS WITH BRAIN DISEASE

The study of Hamsher, Levin, and Benton (1979; Benton, 1980) provides information on the relationship of performance to locus of lesion, aphasic disorder, and visual field defect. The sample consisted of 145 righthanded patients with unilateral focal cerebral lesions. In each case, the lesion was limited to a single quadrant in one hemisphere. The line dividing the anterior from the posterior quadrant was behind the postcentral gyrus and just anterior and superior to Meyer's loop in the temporal lobe. All cases carried a final diagnosis of a unilateral hemispheric lesion which was confirmed by at least one radiographic test (CT scan, brain scan, angiography) or the neurosurgeon's operative report. Additionally, radiographic and neurologic findings had to be congruent, e.g., no case with a lesion in the anterior quadrant was accepted if a visual field defect was present, and similarly, no case localized to the posterior quadrant showed contralateral motor or sensory impairment. Patients with lesions which clinically or radiographically appeared to extend across this anterior–posterior boundary were excluded. Patients were classified according to the presence or absence of aphasia based on neuropsychological test performance and examination of the hospital record. Aphasia was present in 66% of the left hemisphere patients. Aphasic patients were subgrouped according to the presence or absence of significant language comprehension defects, usually as determined by performance on the Token Test or Aural Comprehension of Words and Phrases subtest of the Multilingual Aphasia Examination. Performance or at below the 2nd percentile on either test was considered evidence of defective language comprehension.

Table 4-7 shows the distribution of test scores in the several groups of patients and in normal subjects. Table 4-8 shows the relative frequency of defective performance as defined by a corrected score of less than 38, i.e., a score exceeded by 96.5% of normal subjects. The following points may be made:

1. Among nonaphasic patients, only those with disease of the right hemisphere show an excessively high number of defective performances.

2. Among patients with right hemisphere disease, those with posterior lesions show a higher frequency of defective performance than those with anterior lesions. The difference in the proportion of failures in the two groups (53% vs. 26%) was statistically significant ($p < .05$).

3. Among aphasic patients with left hemisphere disease, only those with substantial impairment in oral language comprehension showed defective facial recognition. In this subgroup, a higher frequency of defect was found in the patients with posterior lesions as compared to those with anterior lesions, but the difference in percentages of failure (44% vs. 29%) was not statistically significant.

4. Of the 36 patients with posterior right hemisphere lesions, 26 had visual field defects. Fifteen (58%) of these 26 patients performed defectively. Four (40%) of the 10 patients with full visual fields performed defectively. This difference in the percentages of patients performing defectively was not statistically significant.

5. Of the 27 aphasic patients with posterior lesions who were impaired in oral language comprehension, 17 had visual field defects. Both these patients and the 10 patients with full visual fields showed about the same relative frequency of defective performance (47% vs. 40%).

6. Among the 22 patients with left hemisphere disease who were not aphasic or whose aphasia was not characterized by substantial impairment in oral language comprehension, 13 (59%) had visual field defects. All performed within normal limits.

7. In a series of eight analyses (within quadrants, hemispheres, total sample, and among aphasic patients), the proportion of defective performances was never different for one sex compared with the other.

The findings of this study differed from those of earlier investigations (including our own) in their indications that there is a subgroup of aphasic patients with impairment in oral language comprehension who perform defectively. The question of why some "sensory" aphasics perform defectively and others do not remains to be resolved. It is clear, however, that among nonaphasic patients with unilateral brain disease, defective performance is associated with lesions of the right hemisphere.

PERFORMANCES OF PSYCHIATRIC PATIENTS

The degree to which facial recognition performance may be affected by functional psychopathology is a question of both theoretical and clinical interest. Some information relevant to the question is provided by the findings of two studies.

In one study (Levin & Benton, 1977), the test was given to 44 patients whose symptoms had raised a question of differential diagnosis between brain disease and functional psychiatric disorder. In every case, the complaints (e.g., defective memory, headache) were sufficiently suggestive of CNS disease to warrant thorough neurological evaluation which, however, disclosed no evidence of such disease and the final diagnosis was some type of functional psychiatric disorder. The findings were that the facial recognition test performances of these patients were indistinguishable from those of normal subjects. The mean score of the group was well within normal limits and the range of scores was comparable to the normal range. Only one patient (finally diagnosed as paranoid schizophrenic with visual hallucinations) performed defectively. Thus the results supported the conclusion that a test of facial recognition could serve as an aid to differential diagnosis of the evaluation of neurologic and "pseudoneurologic" patients.

A second study (Kronfol et al., 1978) assessed facial recognition test performance in 18 psychiatric inpatients suffering from relatively severe depressive illness who were examined directly before the initiation of electroconvulsive therapy. Three (17%) performed defectively (i.e., their scores were exceeded by 96.5% of controls). This indication that the proportion of severely depressed patients with impaired performances was somewhat higher than normal deserves further investigation.

TABLE 4-7   Facial Recognition: Performances of Brain-Diseased Patients

Score	C	RA	RP	LA-NA	LP-NA	LA-A1	LP-A1	LA-A2	LP-A2
53–54	5	–	–	–	1	–	–	–	1
50–52	25	–	1	1	1	–	1	1	1
47–49	46	5	7	4	5	2	2	2	2
44–46	57	3	1	2	5	1	3	–	5
41–43	41	5	3	4	2	1	–	4	4
38–40	14	4	5	4	–	1	2	5	2
35–37	7	2	6	–	–	–	–	2	4
32–34	1	3	11	–	–	–	–	1	2
29–31	–	–	–	–	–	–	–	–	2
26–28	–	1	2	–	–	–	–	1	2
24–25	–	–	–	–	–	–	–	1	2
Total	196	23	36	15	14	5	8	17	27

*C, control subjects; RA, right anterior, nonaphasic; RP, right posterior, nonaphasic; LA-NA, left anterior, nonaphasic; LP-NA, left posterior, nonaphasic; LA-A1, left anterior, aphasic, without comprehension defect; LP-A1, left posterior, aphasic, without comprehension defect; LA-A2, left anterior, aphasic, with comprehension defect; LP-A2, left posterior, aphasic, with comprehension defect.

TABLE 4-8   Facial Recognition: Relative Frequency of Defective Performance

Group	% Defect
Normal subjects (*n*=286)	3.5
Right anterior (*n*=23)	26
Right posterior (*n*=36)	53
Left anterior nonaphasic (*n*=15)	0
Left posterior nonaphasic (*n*=14)	0
Left anterior, aphasic without comprehension defect (*n*=5)	0
Left posterior, aphasic without comprehension defect (*n*=8)	0
Left anterior, aphasic with comprehension defect (*n*=17)	29
Left posterior, aphasic with comprehension defect (*n*=27)	44

PERFORMANCES OF PATIENTS WITH CLOSED HEAD INJURIES

Closed head injury resulting from blunt trauma is often associated with widespread brain damage. One hypothesis about the physiopathologic mechanisms involved is that the neurologic effects are distributed in a centripetal sequence, initially affecting hemispheric structures in preference to mesencephalic brainstem structures. As a partial test of the hypothesis, Levin, Grossman, and Kelly (1977) examined the performances of patients with closed head injuries on the Facial Recognition Test. No patient exceeded 50 years of age and the mean educational level was 10.5 years. They found that patients who were conscious on admission and throughout hospitalization (Grade I severity) did not differ on Facial Recognition Test performance from those who were comatose less than 24 hours (Grade II severity). Defective performances were observed in 12% of such patients. However, defective performance was found in 50% of the patients who were comatose for at least 24 hours (Grade III severity). Classifying patients on the basis of clinical neurologic findings, the authors found that 15% of patients with normal findings and 14% of patients with hemispheric injury but without brainstem involvement performed defectively. Within this combined group, defective performances were more frequent in patients with aphasia (31%) than in nonaphasic patients (4%). However, four out of the five patients with neurologic evidence of brainstem injury in addition to the hemispheric insult performed defectively. Neither the occurrence of depressed skull fracture nor the presence of EEG abnormalities was related to level of performance. The authors concluded that performance on the test "bears a closer relationship to severity of injury as reflected by duration of coma and the full range of neurologic deficits than does the presence of EEG abnormalities." The patients were tested after recovery from the confusional state as reflected by normal performance on a test of orientation. Moreover, defective performances were observed in some outpatients 8–12 months after the date of injury. Thus defective performance in a patient who has sustained a closed head injury is probably a valid behavioral sign of acquired neurologic disability.

REFERENCES

Assal G. (1969) Régression des troubles de la reconnaissance des physionomies et de la mémoire topographique chez un malade opéré d'un hématome intracérébral pariéto-temporal droite. *Rev. Neurol. 121*: 184–185.

Benton A. L. (1980) The neuropsychology of facial recognition. *Am. Psychol. 35*: 176–186.

Benton A. L. & Van Allen M. W. (1968) Impairment in facial recognition in patients with cerebral disease. *Cortex 4*: 344–358.

Benton A. L. & Van Allen M. W. (1972) Prosopagnosia and facial discrimination. *J. Neurol. Sci. 15*: 167–172.

Bodamer J. Die Prosopagnosie (1947) *Arch. Psychiat. Nervenkrank. 179*: 6–54.

Carey S. & Diamond R. (1977) From piecemeal to configurational representation of faces. *Science 195*: 312–314.

De Renzi E., Faglioni P. & Spinnler H. (1968) The performance of patients with unilateral brain damage on facial recognition tasks. *Cortex 4*: 17–34.

Flanagan J. C. (1951) Units, scores and norms. In *Educational Measurement*, E. F. Lindquist (ed). Washington, D.C.: American Council on Education.

Hamsher K., Levin H. S. & Benton A. L. (1979) Facial recognition in patients with focal brain lesions. *Arch. Neurol. 36*: 837–839.

Hécaen H. & Angelergues R. (1962) Agnosia for faces (prosopagnosia). *Arch. Neurol. 7*: 92–100.

Kronfol Z., Hamsher K., Digre K., & Waziri R. (1978) Depression and hemispheric functions: Changes associated with unilateral ECT. *Br. J. Psychiat. 132*: 560–567.

Levin H. S. & Benton A. L. (1977) Facial recognition in "pseudoneurological" patients. *J. Nerv. Ment. Dis. 164*: 135–138.

Levin H. S., Grossman R. G., & Kelly P. J. (1977) Impairment of facial recognition after closed head injuries of varying severity. *Cortex 13*: 119–130.

Levin H. S., Hamsher K. de S. & Benton A. L. (1975) A short form of the Test of Facial Recognition for clinical use. *J. Psychol. 91*: 223–228.

Lhermitte F., Chain F. Escourolle R., Ducarne B. & Pillon B. (1972) Étude anatomo-clinique d'un cas de prosopagnosie. *Rev. Neurol. 126*: 329–346.

Meadows J. C. (1974) The anatomical basis of prosopagnosia. *J. Neurol. Neurosurg. Psychiat. 37*: 489–501.

Pallis C. A. (1955) Impaired identification of faces and places with agnosia for colors. Report of a case due to cerebral embolism. *J. Neurol. Neurosurg. Psychiat. 18*: 218–224.

Quaglino A. & Borelli G. B. (1867) Emiplegia sinistra con amaurosi; guaragione; perdita totale della percezione dei colori e della memoria della configurazione degli oggetti. *Giornale d'Oftalmologia Italiano 10*: 106–117.

Rondot P. & Tzavaras A. (1969) La prosopagnosie après vingt années d'études cliniques et neuropsychologiques. *J. Psychol. Norm. Pathologique 66*: 133–165.

Rondot P., Tzavaras A. & Garcin R. (1967) Sur un cas de prosopagnosie persistant depuis quinze ans. *Rev. Neurol. 117*: 424–428.

Tzavaras A., Hécaen H. & Le Bras H. (1970) Le problème de la spécificité du déficit de la reconnaissance du visage humain lors les lésions hémisphériques unilatérales. *Neuropsychol. 8*: 403–416.

Tzavaras A., Merienne L. & Masure M. C. (1973) Prosopagnosie, amnésie et troubles de langage par lésion temporale gauche chez un sujet gaucher. *Encéphale 62*: 383–394.

Warrington E. K. & James M. (1967) An experimental investigation of facial recognition in patients with unilateral cerebral lesions. *Cortex 3*: 317–326.

5. Judgment of Line Orientation

BACKGROUND

For over a century it has been recognized that disturbances of spatial perception and orientation are among the salient behavioral consequences of brain disease, particularly disease of the right hemisphere. Early case reports by Jackson (1876), Badal (1888), Foerster (1890), Dunn (1895), and Peters (1896) firmly established visual disorientation as a specific symptom of cerebral dysfunction. Dunn went so far as to postulate the existence of a "geographic centre" in the right hemisphere for what he called "the sense of location." Detailed accounts of the history of this topic can be found in the reviews by Critchley (1953), Faust (1955), Ajuriaguerra and Hécaen (1960), Hécaen and Angelergues (1963), Gloning (1965), and Benton (1969, 1972, 1982).

A great variety of test and procedures have been devised to assess different aspects of "spatial thinking." The tests of Thurstone (1938, 1944), visuoconstructive tests (Benton, 1962; Benton & Fogel, 1962), the Minnesota Paper Form Board (Likert & Quasha, 1948), and memory-for-designs tests (Graham & Kendall, 1960; Benton, 1974) are some well-known examples. In addition, spatial thinking is an important component of performance on some tests, such as the Progressive Matrices of Raven (1938) and the Block Designs of Kohs (1923) and Wechsler (1955), that purport to be measures of general intelligence.

The test described below would seem on a priori grounds to be as pure a measure of one aspect of spatial thinking as could be conceived. The impetus for its development as a clinical instrument came from the findings of experimental studies on the perception of line direction in both normal subjects and patients with brain disease. One such study was that of Fontenot and Benton (1972) who investigated the performances of righthanded university students in identifying the direction of lines presented tachistoscopically to the left and right visual fields. The subjects showed a significant left field superiority in perceptual accuracy, thus implicating the right cerebral hemisphere as playing a distinctively important role in the mediation of performance on this spatial task. Warrington and Rabin (1970) compared the performances of patients with unilateral brain disease in judging whether or not pairs of lines differed in slope and found that the mean error score was significantly higher for patients with right hemisphere lesions than for those with left hemisphere lesions or for a control group. Patients with right parietal lesions showed particularly severe impairment. The patients with left hemisphere lesions and the control patients did not differ significantly in performance level.

Benton, Hannay, and Varney (1975) then pursued this line of inquiry by studying the performances of patients with unilateral disease on a more complex task requiring the identification of two simultaneously presented lines of different slope as well as of single lines. The question raised was whether or not this more demanding task might separate unilateral groups even more sharply than had the simple task employed by Warrington and Rabin. The stimuli were presented tachistoscopically to central vision for 300 milliseconds after which the patient identified the lines on a multiple choice response card. A striking interhemispheric difference in performance was found. Thirteen (59%) of the 22 patients with right hemisphere lesions performed defectively (below the poorest score in the control group) while none of the 21 patients with left hemisphere lesions made defective scores. The findings were impressive enough to encourage an effort to develop a procedure that would not require tachistoscopic presentation and that could be used conveniently in the examining room or at the bedside. However, when the experimental task was presented to patients under a condition of unlimited exposure time, it proved to be too easy, and the majority of patients made perfect or near-perfect performances. It was then found that if the stimulus lines were reduced to one-half the length of the lines on the multiple-choice response card, the difficulty of this matching task was augmented to a level comparable to that of the experimental tachistoscopic task. Therefore a procedure requiring the matching of "partial" lines (1.9 cm in length) to "full-length" lines (3.8 cm in length) on the response card was developed and normative standards of performance established (Benton, Varney & Hamsher, 1978).

DESCRIPTION

Two forms of the test, Form H and Form V, consist of the same 30 items presented in a somewhat different order. However, in the case of each form, the items are presented in a generally ascending order of difficulty. The test materials of each form are spiral-bound in a single booklet consisting of 35 stimuli appearing in the upper part of the booklet and the same multiple-choice response card appearing in the lower part. The first five items are practice items. Following this are the 30 test items. The practice items are the same for both forms of the test. Record sheets for each form of the test facilitate recording and scoring.

As will be seen in the booklet, the multiple-choice response card consists of an array of lines, each of which is 1.5 in. (3.8 cm) long, labeled "1" through "11" and drawn at 18-degree intervals from the point of origin.

Each of the five practice items consists of complete reproductions of a pair of full-length lines appearing on the multiple-choice response card. Each of the subsequent 30 test items consists of a pair of partial lines, with each partial line corresponding to the orientation of one of the lines appearing in the multiple-choice response card below it. Each partial line represents, with respect to the origin, either the distal (high), the middle, or the proximal (low) ¾ in. (1.9 cm) segment of a response-choice line.

As indicated on the Record Sheet, there are four types of test stimuli. The HH items consist of two distal line segments. The LL and MM stimulus items consist of two proximal or two middle line segments, respectively. The mixed items (HL, LH, HM, MH, LM) consist of two different line segments.

Corrected split-half reliability of Form H in a sample of 40 subjects was found to be .94. The same statistic for Form V in a sample of 124 subjects was .89. In the combined sample of 164 subjects, the corrected split-half reliability was .91, the standard error of measurement being 1.7. A sample of 37 patients was given both forms of the test, the interval between test and retest ranging from 6 hours to 21 days. The mean scores for the first and second administrations were almost identical (23.1 and 23.5) indicating the absence of a systematic practice effect. The test–retest reliability coefficient was .90 with a standard error of measurement of 1.8 points.

ADMINISTRATION

The test booklet is placed flat on a table in front of the patient with the booklet opened so that the stimulus items in the upper half are positioned at an angle of about 45° with respect to the surface of the table. Generally the booklet should be placed so that the entire response-choice display and stimulus field lie within the area of preserved vision. In any case, the subjects are allowed to hold and position the test booklet to their best advantage.

The examiner should begin with practice item A, point to the lines on the upper stimulus page and say: "*See these two lines? Which two lines down here* (pointing to the response card) *are in exactly the same position and point in the same direction as the two lines up here?*". "*Tell me the number of the lines.*" If the patient supplies the correct answers, say "*That's right*", and proceed with practice item B. If the patient is aphasic or otherwise shows a tendency to misstate the numbers while pointing to the correct response-choices, say instead: "*Show me these lines down here. Point to them.*" If the patient does not understand the task, continue by using your hand to cover the line in position 6 and, pointing to the other line (in position 1), say "*Let us just look at this line. Which line down here* (pointing to the response-choice display) *points in the same direction as this one* (pointing to the stimulus line) *and is also in the same position? That is, it's on the same side of the page as this line up here.*" Record the response on the record sheet where it is labeled A'. Correct the patient if he still supplies the wrong answer and proceed, using these extended instructions, by covering the other line (in position 1) and pointing to the line in position 6. After demonstrating the line in position 6, again supply the correct answers if it is not given on the second trial (A'). Continue with practice item B. If the patient again gives the wrong answers for this practice item, follow up with the extended instructions using single lines (trial B'). Continue with this cycle of instructions until the patient gives two correct responses on the practice items on the first trial. A correct response means identifying *both* response choices for the pair of stimulus lines. If this criterion is not met with at least two practice items, discontinue the test. (See discussion below in the section labeled "Scoring".)

After the five practice items have been presented, and with the test booklet opened to the page labeled "Test Items" say to the patient: "*Now we are going to do more of these, except now the lines which you see up here* (pointing to the upper page) *will be shorter, because part of the line has been erased. Tell me* (show me) *which two lines down here are pointing in the same direction as the lines up here.*"

Do not supply the patient with knowledge of his results on any of the individual test items. However, general statements can be made to provide encouragement and sustain motivation.

If, after 30 seconds, a patient has not given his response choices, he should be encouraged to make his best guess regardless of how uncertain he is about it. There is no time limit for responding. The patient's actual response choice should be entered on the Record Form (not just "right" or "wrong"). Spontaneous corrections by the patient are accepted.

SCORING

After entering the patient's two response choices and examining the correct answers given to the right of the item on the Record Form, circle any errors. At the completion of the test, tally the number of completely correct items and record it. When appropriate, add age and sex corrections as described below.

Patients who fail to meet the pretest criterion on the practice items, i.e., completely correct response choices on the first administration of any two practice items, are classified into one of two categories. Defective performance on the practice items is considered a valid indication of severe impairment in patients who are alert and responsive to the examiner and whose answers, even if incorrect, are appropriate to the instructions. For example, on practice item B where the correct answer is 4 and 8, if the subject gives an erroneous answer, such as 6 and 10, and accurately points to his verbal choices on the response-choice display (or, if nonverbal response choices are being used, the subject can reproduce his same two pointing responses on command) then the answer is considered to be in appropriate form and the performance on this item is considered a valid failure. However, inappropriate responses such as selection of only one or three or more response choices or other responses inappropriate to the instructions (e.g., selecting numbers 16 and 41), the perseveration of the same response choices on consecutive practice items, or failure to make any response choices are considered to be invalid performances in that they probably reflect the presence of confusion, dementia, psychosis, failure to cooperate, impairment in language comprehension, or failure to acquire "test-set," independently of the specific ability to judge line orientation.

In the case of a valid failure to reach criterion on the practice items, a test score of zero is assigned and this is interpreted as severe impairment in the ability to judge line orientation. Failure to reach criterion on the practice items for other (invalid) reasons is not interpreted in relation to the cognitive abilities involved in visuospatial judgments.

NORMATIVE OBSERVATIONS

Inspection of the performances of normal subjects and control patients showed that there was a trend for less well educated subjects to perform less well than the better educated. However, the differences were not consistent from one age-sex group to another. Men under the age of 65 years showed no difference in score related to educational level (12+ years of schooling vs. less than 12 years of schooling) while women, particularly older women, showed more consistent differences. The size of the differences varied widely, no doubt due in part to the small size of some age-sex-education subgroups. The decision was made to ignore the factor of educational level in establishing normative standards until a more substantial mass of data is collected. In contrast, as will be seen, both age and sex exerted a consistent, measurable influence on performance and these factors were taken into account in the standardization.

The test was given to 137 normal subjects or control patients, divided into six age-sex groups. Table 5-1 shows the mean scores of these groups. There is a consistent decline in score of moderate degree with age and there is a consistent difference of about two points between the sexes. Corrections in score that take account of the influence of age and sex were introduced in order to facilitate interpretation of a patient's performance in relation to control subjects of his sex and age. The corrections consisted of adding one point to the obtained scores of subjects in the 50–64 age bracket, three points to the obtained scores of subjects in the 65–74 age bracket, and two points to the obtained scores of women in all age brackets. These corrections resulted in an even level of mean scores across age brackets and sex, the maximal discrepancy being .6 points, as compared to 4.8 points for the uncorrected scores. Table 5-2 shows these mean corrected scores.

The distribution of corrected scores with percentile rank equivalents and a suggested classification are shown in Table 5-3. As will be seen, the test has a relatively low ceiling with 28% of the sample making corrected scores of 29 or 30. Scores of 21 or higher were made by 93% of the sample. Thus it seems reasonable to classify scores of 19 and 20, which are just under the lower limit, as *borderline*, i.e., in the gray zone between clearly defective and very low normal performance. Scores of 17–18, exceeded by 95% of the normative group, are classified as

TABLE 5-1 Judgment of Line Orientation: Mean Raw Scores

Age	Men	Women
16–49 yrs.	25.6 (n=27)	23.3 (n=31)
50–64	24.3 (n=17)	22.2 (n=26)
65–74	22.7 (n=21)	20.8 (n=15)

TABLE 5-2 Judgment of Line Orientation: Mean Corrected Scores*

Age	Men	Women
16–49 yrs.	25.6	25.3
50–74	25.3	25.2
65–74	25.7	25.8

*Score Corrections:
  50–64 years = add 1 point to obtained score
  65–74 years = add 3 points to obtained score
  Women = add 2 points to obtained score

moderately defective, and scores below 17, exceeded by 98.5% of the group, are classified as *severely defective*.

PERFORMANCES OF PATIENTS WITH BRAIN DISEASE

The clinical application of the test was evaluated by giving it to 100 righthanded patients with unilateral brain disease, 50 with left hemisphere lesions, and 50 with right hemisphere lesions. The mean age of the left hemisphere group was 52 years (range = 20–74 years) and mean educational level was 12 years (range = 6–16 years of schooling). Thirty-nine patients (78%) showed one or another type of aphasic disorder. Vascular disease was the most frequent diagnosis (62%); the next most frequent was neoplasms and space-occupying lesions (26%). The mean age of the right hemisphere group was 54 years (range = 22–72 years) and mean educational level was 10.7 years (range = 8–16 years of schooling). None of these patients was aphasic. As in the left hemisphere group, vascular disease was the most frequent

TABLE 5-3   Judgment of Line Orientation: Distribution of Corrected Scores in Normative Sample

Score	Frequency	Percentile	Classification
29–30	38	86+	Superior
27–28	22	72	High average
25–26	22	56	Average
23–24	25	40	Average
21–22	18	22	Low average
19–20	7	9	Borderline
17–18	3	4	Moderately defective
<17	2	1.5	Severely defective

diagnosis (56%), with neoplasms and space-occupying lesions next (42%).

Table 5-4 shows the distributions of corrected scores for these two groups and includes the distribution of scores of the normative sample to facilitate comparisons. It is clear that there is a striking difference in performance level between the right hemisphere group and the other two groups. Among the right hemisphere patients, 46% performed defectively, 10% on a moderately defective level and 36% on a severely defective level. In contrast, only 10% of the left hemisphere patients performed defectively, 8% on a moderately defective level and a single patient (2%) on a severely defective level. Thus the findings provide strong support for the assumption that there is a close association between defective performance and disease of the right hemisphere.

On the basis of radiographic findings and operative reports, it was possible to classify lesions as "prefrontal" (anterior to the precentral gyrus), "Perirolandic" (frontal involving Area 4, frontoparietal, anterior temporal) or "posterior" (parietal behind Areas 1, 2, 3; parieto-occipital; parietotemporal; occipital; posterior temporal) in 31 of the 50 patients with right hemisphere disease. It was not possible to make this determination in the other 19 cases because of radiologic evidence of more than one lesion, a very extensive lesion, or uncertainty about the boundaries of a lesion.

Table 5-5 shows the frequency of failing performances (scores less than 19) of patients in the four categories. The subgroups are further divided into patients with and without visual field defects. The findings indicate that, apart from the indeterminate group, all but two of the failing performances were made by the patients with posterior lesions. This is a very striking finding that on first consideration appears to be too good to be true. Among the cases in the indeterminate category, there were some with lesions not involving the posterior region who performed defectively. However, these were patients with extensive lesions involving both the prefrontal and perirolandic regions. It is evident that the presence or absence of visual field defects is not closely related to performance

**TABLE 5-4   Judgment of Line Orientation: Distribution of
Corrected Scores in Brain-Damaged Patients**

Score	Normative sample (n=137)	Left hemisphere lesions (n=50)	Right hemisphere lesions (n=50)
29–30	38	6	2
27–28	22	11	5
25–26	22	8	3
23–24	25	7	3
21–22	18	9	8
19–20	7	4	6
17–18	3	4	5
<17	2	1	18

level, although there is a slight trend toward a higher frequency of failure in
patients with field defects. Sixteen patients in the left hemisphere group had visual
field defects. Their mean score of 25.0 was in fact slightly higher than the mean
score of 24.1 made by the 34 patients without visual field defects.

Since there was a higher proportion of space-occupying lesions in the right
hemisphere group than in the left hemisphere group (42% vs. 26%), the
performances of the space-occupying and vascular cases were compared to

**TABLE 5-5   Judgment of Line Orientation: Frequency of Failure in
Patients with Right Hemisphere Lesions**

Group	n	No. failures	% Failure
Prefrontal	4	0	–
VDF+*	0	–	–
VFD–*	4	–	–
Perirolandic	15	2	13%
VFD+	3	0	–
VFD–	12	2	17%
Posterior	12	9	75%
VFD+	9	7	78%
VFD–	3	2	67%
Indeterminate	19	12	63%
VFD+	8	6	75%
VFD–	11	6	55%

*VFD+ = visual field defect
 VFD– = no visual field defect

determine whether the observed between-hemispheres difference in scores was ascribable in part to a difference in type of lesion. The findings were negative. In the right hemisphere group, the mean score of the 28 vascular cases was 18.1 and the mean score of the 21 cases with space-occupying lesions was 16.6, the difference between the means being nonsignificant. Forty-three percent of the vascular patients performed defectively as compared to 48% of the patients with space-occupying lesions. In the left hemisphere group, the mean score of the 31 vascular cases was 23.9 while the mean score of the 13 cases with space-occupying lesions was 25.0.

It should be emphasized that these results were obtained on patients who were cooperative and understood the test instructions. Aphasic and confused patients who did not meet the pretest criterion on the practice items because of apparent failure to understand the instructions were excluded from consideration. In clinical practice, a fair number of such patients may be encountered and it is important to distinguish between failure in performance attributable to general cognitive incompetence and failure attributable to a specific defect in spatial thinking.

PERFORMANCES OF CHILDREN

The test was given to a sample of 221 children ranging in age from 7 to 14 years in a study by Lindgren and Benton (1980). In the first phase of the study, 154 children in grades 1, 4, and 7 were tested. In the second phase, one year later, 94 of these children (then in grades 2 and 5) were retested and an additional 67 children in grades 3 and 6 were tested. Thus a total of 315 test performances on the 221 children were obtained. The corrected split-half reliability for these 315 observations across all the age levels was found to be .84. Prorated WISC-R Verbal Scale IQs in the sample ranged from 81 to 127 with a mean of 107 (SD = 11). Children whose age was not appropriate for grade placement or whose IQ was less than 80 or above 130 were excluded from the study. The relationship between Verbal Scale IQ and performance on the visuospatial test proved to be quite small. The correlations computed within each age level ranged from −.09 to .42 with the median coefficient being +.15.

Table 5-6 shows the mean test scores of boys and girls at each age level. As will be seen, there is a progressive, although not entirely consistent, increase in score with age in both boys and girls. Average adult performance is reached by the age of 13 years in both sexes. As is the case in adults, males are consistently superior to females.

The Test of Facial Recognition was given to 168 children in this sample (Lindgren, 1977). The partial correlation coefficient between this test and the test of judgment of line orientation with age and Verbal Scale IQ held constant was .27. The small size of the coefficient indicates that there is little common variance in the two performances and that the tests apparently do not assess the same perceptual capacities.

TABLE 5-6   Judgment of Line Orientation: Scores of Children

Age	Boys			Girls		
	n	Mean	(SD)	*n*	Mean	(SD)
7 yrs.	24	16.8	(4.5)	23	15.3	(5.4)
8	23	19.0	(4.3)	27	17.6	(3.7)
9	18	21.7	(4.1)	19	19.7	(4.2)
10	17	20.6	(6.6)	19	19.3	(5.2)
11	20	22.8	(5.3)	24	21.7	(5.1)
12	20	24.7	(3.8)	22	22.7	(4.0)
13	18	26.1	(3.5)	18	22.7	(4.2)
14	13	26.3	(2.7)	10	23.1	(4.0)

REFERENCES

Ajuriaguerra J. M. & Hécaen H. (1960) *Le Cortex* Cérébral. Paris, Masson.

Badal J. (1888) Contribution a l'étude des cécités psychiques: alexie, agraphie, hémianopsie inférieure, trouble du sens de l'espace. *Archives d'ophtalmologie* 8: 97–117.

Benton A. L. (1962) The Visual Retention Test as a constructional praxis task. *Confinia Neurologica 22*: 141–155.

Benton A. L. (1969) Disorders of spatial orientation. In *Handbook of Clinical Neurology*, Vol. 3, P. J. Vinken and G. W. Bruyn (eds). Amsterdam: North-Holland.

Benton A. L. (1972) The "minor" hemisphere. *J. Hist. Med. Allied Sci. 27*: 5–14.

Benton A. L. (1974) *The Revised Visual Retention Test: Clinical and Experimental Applications*. New York: Psychological Corporation.

Benton, A. L. (1982) Spatial thinking in neurological patients. In *Spatial Abilities*, M. Potegal (ed), New York: Academic Press.

Benton A. L. & Fogel M. L. (1962) Three-dimensional constructional praxis. *Arch. Neurol. 7*: 347–354.

Benton A. L., Hannay H. J. & Varney N. R. (1975) Visual perception of line direction in patients with unilateral brain disease. *Neurology 25*: 907–910.

Benton A. L., Varney N. R. & Hamsher K. (1978) Visuospatial judgment: a clinical test. *Arch. Neurol. 35*: 364–367.

Critchley M. (1953) *The Parietal Lobes*. London: Edward Arnold.

Dunn T. D. (1895) Double hemiplegia with double hemianopsia and loss of geographic centre. *Transactions, College of Physicians of Philadelphia 17*: 45–56.

Faust C. (1955) *Die zerebralen Herdstörungen bei Hinterhauptsverletzungen und ihre Beurteilung*. Stuttgart: Georg Thieme.

Foerster R. (1890) Ueber Rindenblindheit. *Graefes Archiv für Ophthalmologie 36*: 94–108.

Fontenot D. J. & Benton A. L. (1972) Perception of direction in the right and left visual fields. *Neuropsychologia 10*: 447–452.

Gloning K. (1965) *Die zerebral bedingten Störungen des räumlichen Sehens und des Raumerlebens*. Wien: W. Maudrich.

Graham F. K. & Kendall B. S. (1960) Memory-for-Designs Test: Revised General Manual. *Percep. Motor Skills 11*: 147–188.

Hécaen H. & Angelergues R. (1963) *La cécité psychique*. Paris: Masson.

Jackson J. H. (1876) Case of large cerebral tumour without optic neuritis and with left hemiplegia and imperception. *Royal Ophthalmic Hospital Reports 8*: 434–444.

Kohs S. C. (1923) *Intelligence Measurement*. New York: Macmillan.

Likert R. & Quasha W. (1948) *The Revised Minnesota Paper Form Board*. New York: Psychological Corporation.

Lindgren S. D. (1977) Spatial perception in children. Ph.D. Dissertation, University of Iowa.

Lindgren S. D. & Benton A. L. (1980) Developmental patterns of visuospatial judgment. *J. Ped. Psychol. 5*: 217–225.

Peters A. (1896) Ueber die Beziehungen zwischen Orientierungsstoerungen und ein und doppelseitige hemianopsie. *Archiv für Augenheilkunde 32*: 175–187.

Raven J. C. (1938) *Progressive Matrices: A Perceptual Test of Intelligence*. London: H. K. Lewis.

Thurstone L. L. (1938) Primary mental abilities. *Psychometric Monographs*, No. 1.

Thurstone L. L. (1944) A factorial study of perception. *Psychometric Monographs*, No. 4.

Warrington E. K. & Rabin P. (1970) Perceptual matching in patients with cerebral lesions. *Neuropsychologia 8*: 475–487.

Wechsler D. (1955) *Manual for the Wechsler Adult Intelligence Scale*. New York: Psychological Corporation.

6. Visual Form Discrimination

BACKGROUND

Clinicians have often observed that some patients with brain disease show impairment in the capacity to discriminate between complex visual stimulus configurations differing in one or another minor characteristic. A number of systematic studies have confirmed the observation. For example, by means of a matching-to-sample procedure, Meier and French (1965) assessed the visual discrimination of complex figures in patients who had undergone resection of either the right or left temporal lobe for relief of psychomotor seizures. The two groups were equated for mean age (31–33 years), mean WAIS IQ (96–97), and mean performance level on the Porteus Mazes (13.3–13.5 years). The tasks presented assessed the ability to discriminate between fragmented concentric circular patterns on the basis of either a rotational or a structural cue that differentiated one pattern from three other identical patterns. It was found that the performances of the patients with right hemisphere excisions were inferior to those of the patients with left hemisphere excisions; the mean error score of the patients with right-hemisphere lesions was 46% higher and the between-groups difference in mean error score was significant at the .01 level. Studying patients with unilateral brain wounds, Newcombe (1969) also found that those with right hemisphere wounds performed at a lower level than those with left hemisphere wounds. Dee (1970), comparing patients with and without visuoconstructive disability, found that defective visual form discrimination was closely associated with failure on the visuoconstructional tests.

DESCRIPTION

This test was designed as a brief, convenient procedure to assess the capacity for complex visual form discrimination. A pilot study of the performances of children on a pool of 64 multiple-choice items yielded estimates of the difficulty level of each item. Sixteen items covering a fairly broad range in terms of difficulty, but

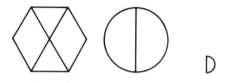

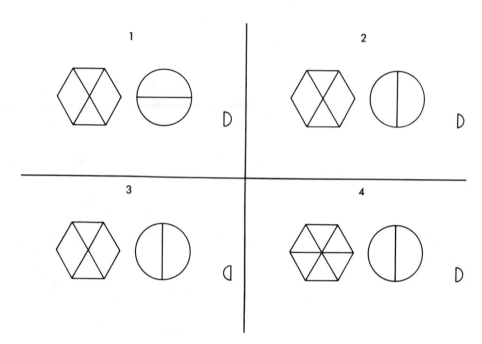

Fig. 6-1   Item 9 of Visual Form Discrimination Test: 1 = rotation of major figure; 2 = correct foil; 3 = rotation of peripheral figure; 4 = distortion of other major figure.

excluding the easiest items, were selected to form this test. Two of the easiest items were selected to serve as demonstration items. One item of the test is shown in Figure 6-1.

Each multiple-choice item includes: (1) the correct foil—C; (2) an incorrect foil involving displacement or rotation of the peripheral figure—PE; (3) an incorrect foil involving rotation of a major figure—MR; (4) an incorrect foil involving distortion of the other major figure—MD. The correct foil appears four times in each of the four positions. On the stimulus designs, the peripheral figure is placed to the left of the major figures in eight designs and to the right of the major figures in the other eight designs. On the multiple choice cards, the incorrect foil involving the peripheral figure consists of its displacement in eight cards and its rotation in the other eight cards.

ADMINISTRATION

The stimulus and the multiple-choice response array are presented simultaneously; the subject's task is to discriminate among the response choices in order to identify the one design that matches the stimulus design.

Demonstration item "A" is presented to the patient, with the multiple-choice card lying flat on the table and the stimulus figure positioned at about 45 degrees to facilitate inspection. For patients with hemianopia or possible neglect of a visual half-field, the booklet should be positioned slightly off the midline in the direction of the intact visual field.

Point to the stimulus design and say, *"See this design? Find it among these four designs"* (pointing to the multiple-choice card). *"Which one is it? Show me."* If the patient responds correctly, either by pointing to or calling the number of the correct foil, confirm the correctness of his response and proceed to demonstration item "B". If he again succeeds, proceed to the test. If he fails either demonstration item, show him the correct foil and point out the difference between it and the foil he chose. Point out the errors on the other two incorrect foils, then proceed to the test.

There is no time limit for the administration of the test. If no response is given after 30 seconds, the patient should be encouraged to make his decision by repeating the question, *"Which one do you think is the same, what is your best guess?"* As long as a patient indicates by his behavior that he is actively working on a decision, e.g., he is systematically matching each figure in the response-choice display to the stimulus figure, he should be allowed to continue. On the other hand, if the patient indicates that he has no idea what the correct response is (e.g., he may say they all look the same to him), then record his response as "No Response." Occasionally a patient may eliminate two response choices and say he is trying to decide between the remaining two, one of which is the correct foil and the other an error foil. If it appears that he has completed his comparison, go on to the next item and record the erroneous foil as his response choice since he could not discriminate it from either the correct foil or the stimulus itself. Thus, if the patient cannot discriminate between the correct foil and a peripheral error (PE), his response is scored as a PE; if he cannot discriminate between a PE and a major distortion (MD), then his response is scored as an MD since this is the more serious error.

SCORING

The scoring system consists of crediting each *correct* response with *2* points and each *peripheral* error response with *1* point. Major rotations, major distortions, and the "no response" error are given *0* credit. Thus, the maximum possible score is 32 and a score of 12 would correspond to a chance level of performance.

TABLE 6-1   Visual Form Discrimination: Means, Medians, and Ranges of Scores in Control Patients

Age	Men	Women
16–54 years	Mean = 30.8 Median = 31.0 Range = 28–32 (*n*=28)	Mean = 29.9 Median = 30.0 Range = 24–32 (*n*=30)
55–75 years	Mean = 29.3 Median = 30.0 Range = 23–32 (*n*=15)	Mean = 30.3 Median = 31.0 Range = 27–32 (*n*=12)

NORMATIVE OBSERVATIONS

A sample of 85 subjects (patients without history or evidence of brain disease or healthy subjects), ranging in age from 19 to 74 years, was given the test. The sample was divided into four subgroups in order to assess the possible influence of age and sex on performance. The performance characteristics of each subgroup are shown on Table 6-1. Since the observed differences among subgroups were small and inconsistent in direction, it was decided that no corrections for age or sex needed to be made.

The possible influence of educational level on performance was evaluated by comparing the scores of the 72 subjects with 12 or more years of schooling to those of the 13 subjects with less than 12 years of schooling. The better educated subgroup had a mean score of 30.1 (range = 24–32) while the less educated subgroup had a mean score of 30.2 (range = 23–32). It was decided that no correction for educational level was indicated.

The distribution of the scores of the 85 control subjects is shown in Table 6-2. As will be seen, a majority of subjects had perfect or near-perfect scores (31–32). Scores of 26 or higher were made by 95% of the group. The score of 23 was made by a 60-year-old man with an 11th grade education. The score of 24 was made by a 42-year-old woman with a 12th grade education.

It seems reasonable to consider a score of 24–25, exceeded by 95% of the sample, as a borderline or mildly defective performance. A score of 23, exceeded by 97% of the sample, may be considered to reflect a moderately defective performance. A score of less than 23 would indicate a severely defective performance.

PERFORMANCES OF PATIENTS WITH BRAIN DISEASE

The test was given to 58 patients, ranging in age from 16 to 68 years, all of whom had definitive diagnoses of hemispheric brain disease. Nineteen patients had lesions of the right hemisphere. Thirty-two patients, 23 of whom were aphasic, had lesions of the left hemisphere. Seven patients had bilateral or diffuse cerebral disease. The distribution of scores of the whole sample is shown in Table 6-2 and the frequency of defective performance in different subgroups is shown in Table 6-3. It will be seen that an extraordinarily high proportion of patients in all the subgroups performed defectively. The large number of patients who showed gross failure (i.e., scores under 20) is particularly noteworthy.

Performance on this task is evidently quite vulnerable to the effects of hemispheric brain disease. Indeed, the high frequency of failure raises the question of the extent to which the test is measuring a specific ability. Since the task does make demands on the capacity for sustained attention, failure may be due to attention-concentration disturbances which are so common in patients with brain disease. This possibility is consonant with the observation that so few patients made perfect or near-perfect performances and that the patients who probably had the most extensive lesions (the bilateral-diffuse subgroup) showed a relatively high frequency of failure. However, other observations support the assumption that performance on the test does measure a specific ability. In line with expectations, the patients with posterior right hemisphere lesions showed the highest frequency of failure among all the subgroups. Moreover, Varney (1981) has found specific relationships between visual form discrimination and certain aspects of aphasic symptomatology. Aphasic alexics (i.e., with severely defective reading comprehension) who still retained the ability to recognize letters showed a 36% frequency of failure on the test of visual form discrimination. In contrast, aphasic alexics with impaired ability to recognize letters showed an 85% frequency of failure on the test. Aphasic patients with only mild impairment in reading comprehension and with intact letter recognition showed only a 13% frequency of failure in visual form discrimination. Varney also has observed that, in the course of recovery from aphasic disorder, improvement in letter recognition is accompanied by a corresponding improvement of performance on the visual form discrimination test.

It is also possible that relative inattention to stimuli in the contralateral visual field (visual neglect) or a more general disturbance in visual search, i.e., defective oculomotor exploration of objects in the visual field, are determinants of failing performance on the test (Heilman, 1979; Tyler, 1969). All these possibilities deserve investigation, in systematic studies as well as in assessing the performance of individual patient. Attention-concentration disturbances should be evident in other performances as well. The presence of unilateral visual neglect should be reflected in a performance pattern that shows a pronounced bias toward selecting foils on only the right or the left side of the page, and it can be assessed

TABLE 6-2   Visual Form Discrimination: Distribution of Scores in Control and Brain-Diseased Patients

	Score													
	32	31	30	29	28	27	26	25	24	23	22	21	20	<20
Control (n=85)	28	17	13	13	4	3	3	2	1	1	–	–	–	–
Brain disease (n=58)	2	6	1	1	6	1	6	2	2	2	4	2	5	18

TABLE 6-3   Visual Form Discrimination: Frequency of Defective Performance*

Group	n	No. defective	% defective
All	58	31	53
Left hemisphere	32	15	47
Right hemisphere	19	11	58
Bilateral-diffuse	7	5	71
Left anterior	12	7	58
Left posterior	15	7	47
Left anterior-posterior	5	1	20
Right anterior	7	3	43
Right posterior	9	7	78
Right anterior-posterior	3	1	33
Left aphasic	23	10	43
Left nonaphasic	9	5	56

*Score of 23 or less

independently by appropriate tests such as the "visual neglect" tests of Albert (1973) and Heilman (1979). Capacity for visual exploration can be assessed by "visual search" tests, such as those of Poppelreuter (1917) and Teuber (1964). Thus the determination of whether or not a failing performance represents a specific disability in visual form discrimination depends on evaluation of the total pattern of test performances.

Clinical Applications   Because of its sensitivity to the effects of brain disease, this brief test had proven to be useful in the clinic when the question of brain disease is raised, particularly in evaluating the possibility of an early dementia. It is also employed as one of a battery of tests for cognitive impairment associated with posterior right hemisphere disease. In the aphasic patient it provides one

TABLE 6-4   Visual Form Discrimination: Record Form

Name _____ No. _____ Date _____

Age _____ Sex _____ Education _____ Handedness _____ Examiner _____

Demonstration Items A _____ (3)   B _____ (3)

Test Items

Item	Correct	Peripheral Error	Major Rotation	Major Distortion	No Response
1.	_____(3)	_____(4)	_____(2)	_____(1)	_____
2.	_____(1)	_____(2)	_____(4)	_____(3)	_____
3.	_____(1)	_____(4)	_____(2)	_____(3)	_____
4.	_____(2)	_____(4)	_____(3)	_____(1)	_____
5.	_____(3)	_____(4)	_____(1)	_____(2)	_____
6.	_____(1)	_____(4)	_____(3)	_____(2)	_____
7.	_____(4)	_____(2)	_____(1)	_____(3)	_____
8.	_____(2)	_____(3)	_____(4)	_____(1)	_____
9.	_____(2)	_____(3)	_____(1)	_____(4)	_____
10.	_____(4)	_____(1)	_____(3)	_____(2)	_____
11.	_____(3)	_____(1)	_____(4)	_____(2)	_____
12.	_____(1)	_____(2)	_____(3)	_____(4)	_____
13.	_____(3)	_____(1)	_____(2)	_____(4)	_____
14.	_____(4)	_____(3)	_____(1)	_____(2)	_____
15.	_____(2)	_____(4)	_____(1)	_____(3)	_____
16.	_____(4)	_____(1)	_____(2)	_____(3)	_____

Totals _____   _____   _____   _____   _____

Observations _____

additional item of information about the extent to which his disabilities extend
beyond the sphere of speech functions.

REFERENCES

Albert M. L. (1973) A simple test of visual neglect. *Neurology 21*: 658–664.

Dee H. L. (1970) Visuoconstructive and visuoperceptive deficits in patients with unilateral cerebral lesions. *Neuropsychologia 8*: 305–314.

Heilman K. M. (1979) Neglect and related disorders. In *Clinical Neuropsychology*, K. M. Heilman & E. Valenstein (eds). New York: Oxford University Press.

Meier M. J. & French L. A. (1965) Lateralized deficits in complex visual discrimination and bilateral transfer of reminiscence following unilateral temporal lobectomy. *Neuropsychologia 3*: 261–272.

Newcombe F. (1969) *Missile Wounds of the Brain*. London: Oxford University Press.

Poppelreuter W. (1917) *Die psychischen Schädigungen durch Kopfschuss im Kriege 1914-1916: die Störungen der niederen und hoheren Sehleistungen durch Verletzungen des Okzipitalhirns.* Leipzig: Voss.

Teuber H-. L. (1964) The riddle of frontal lobe function in man. In *The Frontal Granular Cortex and Behavior*, J. M. Warren & K. Akert (eds). New York: McGraw-Hill.

Tyler H. R. (1969) Defective stimulus exploration in aphasic patients. *Neurology 19*: 105–112.

Varney N. R. (1981) Letter recognition and visual form discrimination in aphasic alexia. *Neuropsychologia 19*: 795–800.

7. Pantomime Recognition

BACKGROUND

Clinicians noted as early in the 1870s that, in addition to their linguistic disturbances, some aphasic patients also showed a failure to understand the meaning of pantomimed actions. Finkelnburg (1870; Duffy and Liles, 1979) regarded the failure as an expression of a general disturbance of symbolic thinking ("asymbolia") which was manifested in an impaired capacity to deal with both linguistic and nonlinguistic information. Hughlings Jackson (1878) and Henry Head (1926) also interpreted defective recognition of pantomimed actions as a basic impairment in symbolic thinking.

Apart from its appearance in the severely demented, defective pantomime recognition is seen predominantly in aphasic patients (cf. Duffy, Duffy & Pearson, 1975; Gainotti & Lemmo, 1976; Varney, 1978). However, only a minority of aphasics show the defect and there is no necessary relationship between the observed severity of an aphasic disorder and incapacity to understand pantomimed actions (cf. Alajouanine & Lhermitte, 1964; Zangwill, 1964; Gainotti & Lemmo, 1976; Varney, 1982).

The status of pantomime recognition in an aphasic patient is of both clinical and theoretical interest. In assessing any aphasic patient, it is worthwhile knowing whether his disability compromises the capacity to understand nonlinguistic as well as linguistic messages. Varney (1978, 1982) found that impaired pantomime recognition was particularly closely related to defective reading comprehension, in contrast to its somewhat weaker association with oral language comprehension and naming ability. Ferro, Santos, Castro-Caldas, and Mariano (1980) have reported similar results. This finding raises the question of the role of sensory modality in defining the performance patterns of individual aphasic patients. There are indications that the status of pantomime recognition may have predictive significance with respect to the rate and extent of recovery from an aphasic disorder; because of its important clinical implications, this possibility deserves to be investigated. The neuropathological basis of defective pantomime recognition remains to be identified both in aphasic and demented patients.

The pantomime recognition test described below was developed to provide an objective, standardized procedure for assessing a patient's ability to understand meaningful, nonlinguistic pantomimed actions. The test requires the patient to point to drawings of objects whose pretended uses are shown in a series of videotaped pantomimes. Because assessment of pantomime recognition is of special interest in aphasic patients, instruction and response procedures have been designed to make minimal demands on linguistic and praxic abilities.

DESCRIPTION

The pantomimes which serve as test stimuli were recorded on a ¾-inch videotape cassette for presentation on a color television monitor. Each pantomime shows a man pretending to use a common object, such as a spoon, pen, or saw, followed by 7 seconds of blank tape. The first four pantomimes are practice items. They were selected because they proved to be quite easy even for most aphasics and were included in order to familiarize the patient with the test requirements and response procedures (cf. Duffy et al., 1975). The remaining 30 pantomimes are the test items.

A booklet of response choices, each page of which contains four line drawings, is presented along with the videotaped pantomimes. The first page, labeled P, is used with the four practice items. The remaining 30 numbered pages are used with each of the test items. The specific drawings on each of the test item response forms have been designed so that four types of response choices are available on each test trial.

1. *Correct Choice:* The object whose use is pantomimed (e.g., a saw).
2. *Semantic Foil:* An object belonging to the same class of objects as the stimulus (e.g., an axe).
3. *Neutral Foil:* An object whose use is pantomimed elsewhere on the test (e.g., a pen).
4. *Odd Foil:* An object whose use is not suitable for pantomime (e.g., a tree).
The 30 test items and their response foils are shown in Table 7-1.

ADMINISTRATION

The patient should be seated at a table with the response booklet in front of him and the television monitor 4 to six feet away at eye level. Be sure that the monitor is properly adjusted and that the patient is wearing his glasses, if indicated. With the response booklet opened to the first page, direct the patient's attention to the television monitor and show the first pantomime. After the pantomime is completed, point to the response booklet and say *"Which one of these things was the man pretending to use? Point to it down here."* If the patient responds correctly, continue with the remaining practice items. If he fails to respond, responds incorrectly, or responds inappropriately (e.g., naming, imitation, etc.), point to the correct response foil and say *"He was pretending to use this one, the comb."* Following this, repeat the first practice item. For some patients, two or three repetitions may be required to establish the appropriate response set. Some improvisation may be required of the examiner in instructing patients.

If a patient responds correctly on three of the four practice items, proceed with the remaining 30 test items. After each pantomime is finished and the patient has responded, turn to the next page of the response booklet. Be careful not to turn the page before the pantomime is finished, even if the patient has already responded, since this confuses some patients.

If a patient responds incorrectly on two or more of the practice items, terminate the test. It may be assumed that he is either severely impaired in pantomime recognition or that he does not understand the test instructions.

SCORING

The test calls for 30 scorable responses. For each test item, indicate the specific response choice made. The record form to be used for this purpose is shown in Table 7-1, in which correct choices, semantic foils, neutral foils, and odd foils are arranged in columns. After the test is completed, tally the number of correct responses and errors of each type. One point is given for each correct response. Since the chance of success by random guessing is one in four, the effective range of scores is 8 to 30 correct.

NORMATIVE OBSERVATIONS

The test was given to 30 hospitalized inpatients (21 men, 9 women) without evidence of past or present brain disease who ranged in age from 38 to 60 years and in educational level from 8 to 16 years. The mean score of the group was 28.7 (range = 26–30). The distribution of the scores is shown in Table 7-2. As will be seen, the majority of patients made perfect or near-perfect performances (scores of 29–30) and two patients made scores of 26. On the basis of these observations, scores of less than 26 were classified as defective.

PERFORMANCES OF PATIENTS WITH BRAIN DISEASE

Aphasia To date, systematic data have been collected only on aphasic patients. The distribution of scores of 105 patients who showed clinically evident aphasic symptomatology and were judged to have lesions confined to the left hemisphere is shown in Table 7-2. About 30% of the group made perfect or near-perfect scores (29–30) and about 60% performed within the normal range. The severity of defect shown by the remaining 41 patients varied widely. At the one extreme, 10 patients could be classified as mildly defective (scores of 24–25) and, at the other extreme,

TABLE 7-1   Pantomime Recognition Test: Record Form

Name _____ No. _____ Date _____
Age _____ Sex _____ Education _____ Handedness _____ Examiner _____

Practice Items

(a) comb _____ (b) rifle _____ (c) sink _____ (d) razor _____

Test Items

	Correct		Semantic		Neutral		Odd
1) ____	(apple)	____	(banana)	____	(sink)	____	(elephant)
2) ____	(saw)	____	(axe)	____	(glass)	____	(train)
3) ____	(cup)	____	(glass)	____	(gun)	____	(church)
4) ____	(ball)	____	(bat)	____	(telephone)	____	(boat)
5) ____	(cigarette)	____	(pipe)	____	(camera)	____	(frog)
6) ____	(violin)	____	(trombone)	____	(gun)	____	(anchor)
7) ____	(toothbrush)	____	(razor)	____	(spoon)	____	(plane)
8) ____	(window)	____	(door)	____	(umbrella)	____	(clock)
9) ____	(knife)	____	(spoon)	____	(bat)	____	(church)
10) ____	(binoculars)	____	(camera)	____	(hammer)	____	(horse)
11) ____	(needle)	____	(iron)	____	(door)	____	(penny)
12) ____	(tie)	____	(shoe)	____	(saw)	____	(leaf)
13) ____	(pipe)	____	(cigarette)	____	(camera)	____	(frog)
14) ____	(telephone)	____	(T.V.)	____	(axe)	____	(frog)
15) ____	(spoon)	____	(knife)	____	(bat)	____	(boat)
16) ____	(hammer)	____	(brush)	____	(pipe)	____	(target)
17) ____	(banana)	____	(apple)	____	(sink)	____	(elephant)
18) ____	(glass)	____	(cup)	____	(gun)	____	(church)
19) ____	(bat)	____	(ball)	____	(telephone)	____	(boat)
20) ____	(gun)	____	(rifle)	____	(cigarette)	____	(leaf)
21) ____	(door)	____	(window)	____	(umbrella)	____	(clock)
22) ____	(brush)	____	(hammer)	____	(pipe)	____	(target)
23) ____	(trombone)	____	(piano)	____	(brush)	____	(anchor)
24) ____	(iron)	____	(needle)	____	(door)	____	(penny)
25) ____	(pen)	____	(typewriter)	____	(tie)	____	(mail box)
26) ____	(candle)	____	(bulb)	____	(pen)	____	(mail box)
27) ____	(piano)	____	(trombone)	____	(brush)	____	(anchor)
28) ____	(umbrella)	____	(tent)	____	(razor)	____	(plane)
29) ____	(axe)	____	(saw)	____	(glass)	____	(train)
30) ____	(camera)	____	(binoculars)	____	(hammer)	____	(horse)

Total:____   ____   ____   ____

Notes: _____
_____
_____

TABLE 7-2 Pantomime Recognition: Distributions of Scores in Control and Aphasic Patients

Score	Controls (n=30)	Aphasics (n=105)
30	11	18
29	7	15
28	7	14
27	3	9
26	2	8
25		7
24		3
23		4
22		4
21		5
20		1
19		2
18		3
17		4
16		2
15		2
14		1
13		0
12		1
11		1
10		1

17 patients could be classified as severely defective (scores of 10–19).

The errors made by most aphasic patients who show defective pantomime recognition are predominantly of the semantic type rather than of the neutral or odd types. In a study of 40 patients whose test scores ranged from 10 to 25, Varney and Benton (1982) found that 36 made a greater number of semantic errors than of neutral and odd errors combined. The performance pattern in 17 cases was characterized by 4–10 semantic errors in combination with not more than one other error. All four patients who showed a frequency of semantic errors of less than 50% were grossly impaired in pantomime recognition with scores ranging from 11 to 16. Yet other grossly impaired patients made a very high proportion of semantic errors. For example, one patient (score = 12) made 16 semantic errors, one neutral error, and one odd error. Another patient (score = 15) made 13 semantic errors, one neutral error, and one odd error. Still another patient (score = 16) made 12 semantic errors, one neutral error, and one odd error. Thus, although a sizable number of neutral and odd errors are made only by patients with severely defective pantomime recognition, other patients who are equally defective make virtually only semantic errors.

This finding that most aphasic patients with defective pantomime recognition show a marked response bias in favor of semantic errors suggests that their failing performance is due to a semantically vague understanding of the significance of the. pantomimed actions rather than to confusion or complete lack of understanding. An analogy can be drawn between their responses in interpreting the nonverbal messages from pantomimed actions and their imprecise understanding of verbal messages when they fail to make correct choices among objects within the same category, e.g., knife for fork, crayon for pencil. The studies of Vignolo (1969; Spinnler & Vignolo, 1966) on sound recognition in aphasic patients illustrate the same point. The majority of errors made by these patients in identifying nonverbal sounds consisted of choosing incorrect foils that are semantically related to the correct choice (e.g., cock crowing for canary singing, cat meowing for dog barking), rather than acoustically similar foils (e.g., man whistling for canary singing) or irrelevant foils.

The question arises as to whether defective pantomime recognition in aphasic patients is merely a reflection of a pervasive general mental impairment. The observations of Varney (1982) on the WAIS Block Design performances of aphasics with impaired pantomime recognition suggest that this is not the case. The range of age-corrected scale scores in a group of 18 such patients was 0–14 with five patients making scores of 10 or higher. In contrast, 17 of the 18 patients failed a simple test of reading comprehension. The exceptional case obtained a score of 25 in pantomime recognition (i.e., one point below the normal range) and a score of 16 on the reading comprehension test (i.e., at the 5th percentile of the normal distribution).

Nonaphasic Patients Only scattered observations have been made on the performances of nonaphasic patients. Failing performance is not rare among demented patients and is occasionally encountered in patients with focal brain disease. The correlates of performance level in these patients remain to be identified.

REFERENCES

Alajouanine T. & Lhermitte F. (1964) Non-verbal communication in aphasia. In *Disorders of Language*, A. De Reuck & M. O'Connor (eds). Boston: Little Brown.

Duffy R., Duffy J. & Pearson K. (1975) Pantomime recognition in aphasic patients. *J. Speech Hearing Res. 18*: 115–132.

Duffy R. & Liles B. Z. (1979) Finkelnburg's 1870 lecture on aphasia with commentary. *J. Speech Hearing Dis. 44*: 156–168.

Ferro J., Santos M., Castro-Caldas A. & Mariano G. (1980) Gesture recognition in aphasia. *J. Clin. Neuropsychol. 3*: 277–292.

Finkelnburg C. F. (1870) Niederrheinische Gesellschaft: Sitzung von 21 März 1870 in Bonn. *Berliner Klinischer Wochenschrift 7*: 449–450; 460–462.

Gainotti G. & Lemmo M. (1976) Comprehension of symbolic gestures in aphasia. *Brain and Language 3*: 451–460.

Head H. (1926) *Aphasia and Kindred Disorders of Speech*, London: Cambridge University Press.

Jackson J. H. (1878) On affections of speech from disease of the brain. *Brain 1*: 304–330.

Spinnler H. & Vignolo L. A. (1966) Impaired recognition of meaningful sounds in aphasia. *Cortex 2*: 337–348.

Varney N. R. (1978) Linguistic correlates of pantomime recognition in aphasic patients. *J. Neurol. Neurosurg. Psychiat. 41*: 564–568.

Varney N. R. (1982) Pantomime recognition defect in aphasia: implications for the concept of asymbolia. *Brain and Language 15*: 32–39.

Varney N. R. & Benton A. L. (1982) Qualitative aspects of pantomime recognition in aphasia. *Brain and Cognition 1*: 132–139.

Vignolo L. A. (1969) Auditory agnosia: a review and report of recent evidence. In *Contributions to Clinical Neuropsychology*, A. L. Benton (ed). Chicago: Aldine Press.

Zangwill O. L. (1964) Intelligence in aphasia. In *Disorders of Language*, A. De Reuck & M. O'Connor (eds). Boston: Little Brown.

8. Tactile Form Perception

BACKGROUND

It had been known for centuries that disease of the nervous system could produce "sensory paralysis," i.e., raised thresholds for pressure, pain, and thermal stimuli. "Higher level" impairment in tactile discrimination and recognition within a setting of apparently adequate basic sensory capacity first engaged the attention of physicians in the last decades of the 19th century, a period of intense interest in the specific symptomatology associated with focal brain disease. It was at this time that "astereognosis," i.e., inability to recognize objects by tactile-kinesthetic exploration, was definitively described by Hoffmann (1885) and Wernicke (1895). Impairment in spatial discrimination, as reflected in raised two-point thresholds and inaccurate location of tactile stimulation of the body surface, was also investigated. There was a gradual accumulation of evidence indicating that these defects could be shown in the absence of more basic sensory loss and, conversely, that patients with raised thresholds for pressure, pain and temperature could retain intact localizing capacity (cf. Foerster, 1901). At the same time, the importance of intact proprioceptive sensitivity in the mediation of successful tactile recognition and discrimination was emphasized by some investigators. The observation was made that patients could show dissociated defects, e.g., defective object recognition with intact spatial discrimination or vice versa.

It was recognized that these disturbances in tactile recognition and discrimination could occur with disease at any level of the nervous system from the peripheral nerves to the cerebral cortex. In patients with hemispheric brain disease, it was generally (but not universally) agreed that the mechanisms mediating these performances were primarily located in the parietal lobes and that failure on tactile recognition and discriminative tasks was a sensitive indicator of the presence of disease in this region.

Wernicke distinguished two stages in tactile object recognition, one of "primary" identification in which the somesthetic information was integrated into a clear unitary percept and one of "secondary" identification in which the object is recognized as such through association with past experience. Other authors (e.g.,

Delay, 1935) presented more detailed analyses. The role of primary sensory defect, particularly of the proprioceptive system, in producing "higher-level" disturbances of discrimination and recognition has been debated for decades and the question is still not resolved. One reason for the lack of agreement is conflicting terminology: diverse performances at different levels of complexity, which make demands on different abilities, are covered by such terms as "astereognosis," "tactile agnosia," "tactile amnesia," and "tactile asymboly," all of which have been applied to the entire spectrum of defects. Moreover, widely different tasks have been utilized to assess tactile discrimination and recognition, e.g., object naming, object matching, recognition of two-dimensional and three-dimensional geometric figures, and recognition of numbers or letters drawn on the surface of the skin ("graphesthesis"). The test described below is in no sense a measure of tactile recognition "in general." It assesses only a single aspect of tactile information processing, and level of performance on the test has distinctive correlates and implications.

DESCRIPTION

The test was originally designed to assess nonverbal tactile information processing in patients who failed tactile object naming and tactile object matching tests. It was anticipated that the performance level would provide a clue as to whether or not failure on the naming and matching tasks was determined by a perceptual disability. Later the test found wider application when it became apparent that failing performance was associated with other indications of impaired "spatial thinking" in patients with brain disease.

The test consists of two parallel sets of 10 cards, each of which presents a geometric figure made of fine-grade sandpaper. The subject is instructed to use the right or left hand to feel the figure (which is concealed from view by a box) and to identify it from visual inspection of a multiple-choice card containing 12 ink line drawings of the figures, slightly reduced in size. Thirty seconds are allowed to explore each figure and the subject is required to respond within 45 seconds. The parallel sets (designated as Forms A and B) are of equivalent difficulty. A practice card is presented before the test is given in order to familiarize the subject with the nature of the task. The arrangement for testing is illustrated in Figure 8-1.

ADMINISTRATION

The subject is seated before the box (which has a slanted top and an open side through which he may place his hand). The examiner is seated across a table from the subject. The ten cards with sandpaper figures are placed in order in the box and the examiner says:

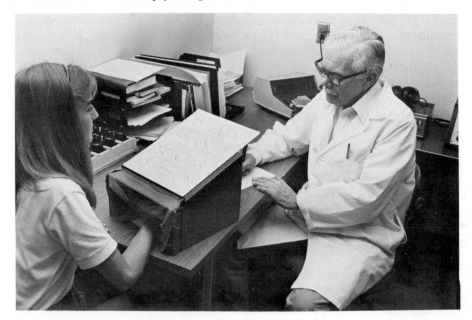

Fig. 8-1   Arrangement for testing tactile form perception.

> *"Now I want to see how good you are at finding out what I put in this box
> by feeling it with your fingers. I will put some sandpaper figures on cards in
> the box. The figures look like the ones on this card here."*

Examiner places the multiple-choice card on the slanted top of the box. Then he
places the practice card in the box and says:

> *"Feel around and touch all parts of this card so that you won't miss
> anything."*

As the subject explores the card, say:

> *"Now, can you show me which figure it was? Point to the figure on this
> card which is the same as the one in the box."*

If he is not handicapped by motor disability, the subject is instructed to use his
other hand to point to the figure on the multiple-choice card. If motor disability
makes this impossible, he is instructed to withdraw his hand from the box and
point to the figure.

If the subject does not identify the figure correctly, the trial is repeated while the
examiner points to the correct figure on the multiple-choice card.

Continue the test by saying:

"Place your hand in the box and feel the next figure there. Make sure that you have touched all the parts before you make your choice. After you have felt the whole card I want you to point to the figure on this board which is the same shape as the figure you just felt. If you don't know for sure, make a guess."

Time is taken with a stopwatch or a sweep second hand.

As soon as a choice has been made, whether correct or incorrect, the card is withdrawn and placed face down beside the examiner. The next card is now in place in the box. Allow the subject a maximum of 30 seconds to feel the card; then tell him that he must make a choice. If he does not give an answer within the next 15 seconds, encourage him to guess. If he fails to respond, the card is removed and the next item is presented.

The examiner presents each succeeding card by saying:

"Here is another figure for you to feel. Once again, feel the whole card."

When the subject has finished the test, present the second set of sandpaper cards and the corresponding multiple-choice display and proceed with the opposite hand in the same way if motor or sensory disability does not prevent testing that hand. Patients with moderate sensory disability are usually testable. However, even moderate motor disability often prevents adequate exploration of the figures. Testing is restricted to the unaffected hand in these cases.

SCORING

Score each response for correctness and identify specific incorrect responses on the record form (Table 8-1). Sum the scores for each hand separately and for both hands together. The examiner may wish to record the time taken until a response is made.

EQUIVALENT FORMS

The relative difficulty level of Forms A and B was assessed by testing a sample of 56 right-handed normal subjects divided into four subgroups of 14 subjects each (4 men, 10 women) who received the tests in the following orders: group 1—right hand, Form A followed by left hand, Form B; group 2—left hand, Form A followed by right hand, Form B; group 3—right hand, Form B followed by left hand, Form A; group 4—left hand, Form B followed by right hand, Form A. The mean scores of the 56 subjects for this counterbalanced administration were 9.12 for Form A and 8.95 for Form B, indicating that the forms are of essentially equivalent difficulty. No influence of hand preference on performance was evident (mean score for right hand = 9.00; mean score for left hand = 9.07). Nor did order

TABLE 8-1   Tactile Form Perception: Record Form

Name _____ No. _____ Date _____

Age _____ Sex _____ Education _____ Handedness _____ Examiner _____

Form A	**Form B**
Hand Used _____	Hand Used _____

D-1 _____ Z   D-1 _____ Ѳ

RESPONSE   RESPONSE

A-1 _____ △   B-1 _____ □

A-2 _____ ○   B-2 _____ +

A-3 _____ ▭   B-3 _____ M

A-4 _____ ⬭   B-4 _____ ⬀

A-5 _____ ◇   B-5 _____ ♡

A-6 _____ 人   B-6 _____ ◳

A-7 _____ 8   B-7 _____ ♀

A-8 _____ ✕   B-8 _____ [ ]

A-9 _____ ♡   B-9 _____ ⊗

A-10 _____ ☆   B-10 _____ ⊠

SCORE _____ / 10   SCORE _____ / 10

OBSERVATIONS:

_____

of presentation have a significant effect on performance (mean score for first test = 8.98; mean score for second test = 9.08).

NORMATIVE OBSERVATION ON ADULTS

The tests were given to 90 normal subjects (41 men, 49 women) in the age range 15–70 years. All but one subject were right-handed. Table 8-2 shows the mean score and range of scores for each hand and both hands in three age groups: 15–50 years; 51–60 years; 61–70 years.

Inspection of the table indicates that there is a slight decline in mean score with advancing age. The poorest score on either hand was 6, which was made by two

TABLE 8-2 Tactile Form Perception: Normal Adult Performance

Men

	15–50 years (n=27)			51–60 years (n=8)			61–70 years (n=6)		
	R.H.	L.H.	B.H.	R.H.	L.H.	B.H.	R.H.	L.H.	B.H.
Mean	9.63	9.70	19.25	9.13	9.13	18.25	9.00	9.33	18.33
Range	6–10	8–10	14–20	7–10	8–10	16–20	7–10	8–10	16–20

Women

	15–50 years (n=15)			51–60 years (n=8)			61–70 years (n=26)		
	R.H.	L.H.	B.H.	R.H.	L.H.	B.H.	R.H.	L.H.	B.H.
Mean	9.93	9.67	19.60	9.00	9.13	18.13	8.96	9.04	18.00
Range	9–10	8–10	17–20	7–10	8–10	15–20	6–10	8–10	15–20

R.H. = right hand, L.H. = left hand, B.H. = both hands.

subjects, a 45-year-old male high school graduate (right-hand score = 6; left-hand score = 8) and a 63-year-old woman with a tenth grade education (right-hand score = 6; left-hand score = 9). The next poorest score of 7 was made by three subjects (ages 52, 60, and 69). Thus one (2.4%) of the 42 subjects under the age of 51 and one (2.1%) of the 48 subjects in the age range 51–70 years made a score of 6, i.e., 2.2% of the total sample of 90 subjects. Hence a score of 6 or less on either hand was classified as a defective performance. Although none of the 42 subjects in the 15–50 years group made a score of 7, this score was made by three of the 48 subjects in the 51–70 years group, i.e., a relative frequency of 3.3% for the total sample. On this basis, a score of 7 was classified as reflecting borderline performance.

The lowest total score for both hands was 14, made by the 45-year-old man whose score with the right hand was 6. The next lowest score of 15 was made by two subjects, a 60-year-old female high school graduate and the 63-year-old woman whose score with the right hand was 6. Four subjects had scores of 16. On this basis, a "both hands" score of 14 was classified as clearly defective and a "both hands" score of 15 as borderline defective.

The largest difference in score between the hands was three points, made by the 63-year-old woman who performed defectively with the right hand. Eight subjects showed a difference of two points between left-hand and right-hand scores. On this basis, a "difference" score between the hands of 3 was classified as reflecting a significant dissociation between right- and left-hand performances.

The normative findings are summarized in Table 8-3, which gives the distributions of the several scores.

PERFORMANCES OF ELDERLY SUBJECTS

The tests were given to 25 subjects (8 men, 17 women) in the 71–80 age range. The mean score for each hand and for both hands combined are shown in Table 8-4. Comparisons with the performances of the younger age groups (Table 8-2) indicate a small decline in performance level in the older group, amounting to about one point in mean score for each hand. Two (8%) of the 25 subjects made single-hand scores of 6, as compared to 2.2% of the younger sample. Two subjects (8%) made single-hand scores of 7, as compared to 3.3% of the younger sample. Three older subjects (12%) made total scores of 14–15, as compared to 3.3% of the younger sample. Only one subject (4%) showed a difference of 3 points in score between the hands.

PERFORMANCE PATTERNS

A number of performance patterns have been defined on the basis of the normative data (Table 8-5).

TABLE 8-3 Tactile Form Perception: Distributions of Scores*

	Single-hand			Combined	
Score	Right hand	Left hand		Score	Both hands
10	59	54		20	41
9	21	26		19	26
8	5	10		18	12
7	3	–		17	4
				16	4
6	2	–		15	2
				14	1

*90 normal subjects, age range 15–70 years.

TABLE 8-4 Tactile Form Perception: Performances of Older Subjects*

	Single-hand			Combined	
Score	Right hand	Left hand		Score	Both hands
10	10	9		20	4
9	7	7		19	7
8	8	5		18	5
7	–	2		17	4
6	–	2		16	2
				15	1
				14	2

*Twenty-five normal subjects, age range 71–80 years.

TABLE 8-5 Tactile Form Perception: Performance Patterns

A. *Normal.* Total score = 16–20; difference between single-hand scores 0–2 points.

B. *Borderline.* Total score = 15; difference between single-hand scores = 0–2 points.

C. *Bilateral symmetric defect.* Total score = 0–14; difference between single-hand scores = 0–2 points; single-hand scores 0–7.

D. *Bilateral asymmetric (right hand) defect.* Total score = 3–11; single-hand scores = 0–7; right-hand score 3 points lower than left-hand score.

E. *Bilateral asymmetric (left hand) defect.* Total score 3–11; single-hand score 0–7; left-hand score 3 points lower than right-hand score.

F. *Right unilateral defect.* Total score = 8–17; right-hand score 3 or more points lower than left-hand score of 8–10.

G. *Left unilateral defect.* Total score = 8–17; left-hand score 3 or more points lower than right-hand score of 8–10.

AR. *Normal right hand.* Right-hand score = 8–10; left hand not tested.

AL. *Normal left hand.* Left-hand score = 8–10; right hand not tested.

BR. *Borderline right.* Right-hand score = 7; left hand not tested.

BL. *Borderline left.* Left-hand score = 7; right hand not tested.

(F). *Right-hand defect.* Right-hand score = 0–6; left hand not tested.

(G). *Left-hand defect.* Left-hand score = 0–6; right hand not tested.

NORMATIVE OBSERVATIONS ON CHILDREN

The study of Spreen and Gaddes (1969) provides normative data on the performances of school children in the age range of 8–14 years. The sample of 404 children tested (200 boys, 204 girls) was a random selection of children in the school system of Victoria, British Columbia. The only criteria for exclusion were that children who had repeated a grade or who were known to have learning problems, conduct disorders, or "brain dysfunction" were not included in the study. The mean IQ of this sample was about 112, which was close to a previously determined IQ of 109 for children in the Victoria school district.

The children were tested first on Form A with their preferred hand, followed by Form B with their nonpreferred hand. Since there is no record of which hand was preferred, the number of children who showed left-hand preference is not known. The scores for each hand were analyzed separately. Total scores for both hands were not recorded.

Tables 8-6 and 8-7 show the mean scores of the boys and girls in each age group for the preferred and nonpreferred hand. No noteworthy sex differences are apparent. The mean scores of the boys and the girls for all age groups were very similar for both the preferred and nonpreferred hands and the direction of the sex differences in score from one age group to another was inconsistent. Overall, there was a slight superiority in performance with the preferred hand on Form A as compared to performance with the nonpreferred hand on Form B. As indicated in the tables, there was a difference between the preferred and nonpreferred hands of .21 points for the boys, a difference of .39 points for the girls, and a difference of .30 points for the combined group.

There was the expected rise in performance level with increasing age. However, there were some reversals in mean score between adjacent age groups which are possibly attributable to the small sample size in some age groups. For this reason, adjacent age groups were combined in forming score distributions to establish normative values, as shown in Table 8-8.

As Table 8-8 shows, performance levels vary widely (particularly for the nonpreferred hand) in children below the age of 12 years. The children in the 12–14 years age range show a much narrower range of scores and the cutting scores developed for adults (i.e., 7 = borderline; below 7 = defective) can be applied to their performances.

PERFORMANCES OF PATIENTS WITH BRAIN DISEASE

Table 8-9 shows the performance patterns in a sample of 104 patients (56 men, 48 women) with brain disease divided into categories according to locus of lesion, presence or absence of aphasia, and presence or absence of motor or sensory defect. The patients ranged in age from 18 to 69 years. Four of the 104 patients were left-handed or ambidextrous. None of the patients with lesions of the right

TABLE 8-6 Tactile Form Perception: Performances of Children on Form A with Preferred Hand*

Age, years	Boys (n)	Mean score	SD	Girls (n)	Mean score	SD	Combined (n)	Mean score	SD
8	(16)	8.4	1.2	(21)	7.6	1.5	(37)	8.0	1.4
9	(44)	7.8	1.3	(42)	8.7	1.2	(86)	8.2	1.3
10	(45)	8.7	1.1	(45)	8.6	1.3	(90)	8.7	1.2
11	(34)	9.2	1.0	(27)	8.3	1.1	(61)	8.8	1.1
12	(24)	9.3	.9	(24)	9.3	1.0	(48)	9.3	.9
13	(16)	9.2	1.0	(22)	9.6	1.1	(38)	9.4	1.0
14	(21)	9.4	.9	(23)	9.7	.8	(44)	9.5	.9
Overall mean		8.75			8.79			8.77	

*Adapted from Spreen and Gaddes (1969)

TABLE 8-7 Tactile Form Perception: Performances of Children on Form B with Nonpreferred Hand*

Age, years	Boys (n)	Mean score	SD	Girls (n)	Mean score	SD	Combined (n)	Mean score	SD
8	(16)	8.1	1.5	(21)	8.2	1.3	(37)	8.2	1.3
9	(44)	7.9	1.4	(42)	8.0	1.5	(86)	7.9	1.4
10	(45)	8.0	1.4	(45)	7.7	1.5	(90)	7.9	1.4
11	(34)	9.0	1.2	(27)	7.8	1.5	(61)	8.5	1.4
12	(24)	9.3	.9	(24)	9.4	.9	(48)	9.4	.9
13	(16)	8.8	1.3	(22)	9.3	1.2	(38)	9.1	1.2
14	(21)	9.6	.8	(23)	9.5	.9	(44)	9.5	.9
Overall mean		8.54			8.40			8.47	

*Adapted from Spreen and Gaddes (1969)

TABLE 8-8   Tactile Form Perception in Children: Score Distributions

	Age, years							
	8–9		10–11		12–13		14	
Score	P	NP	P	NP	P	NP	P	NP
10	35	33	62	40	52	48	29	31
9	29	26	32	42	18	19	11	7
8	16	22	28	22	12	15	2	5
7	25	16	18	14	3	3	2	1
6	9	13	9	15	–	–	–	–
5	7	7	1	8	1	–	–	–
4	1	4	1	6	–	1	–	–
3	1	4	–	1	–	–	–	–
2	–	–	–	3	–	–	–	–

P = preferred hand, NP = nonpreferred hand.

hemisphere were aphasic. All but two of the patients with unilateral lesions had vascular or neoplastic disease; the exceptional cases had atrophic lesions. In the bilateral group, 8 patients had degenerative disease, 2 had vascular disease, 1 had neoplastic disease, and 1 had sustained head trauma. Seventy-five patients had both hands tested. Testing was restricted to one hand for the remaining 29 patients because of motor or sensory defect.

The following observations may be made from Table 8-9.

1. The overall frequency of abnormal performance patterns is quite high. Among the 75 patients who had both hands tested, only 33 (44%) performed at a normal level. Of the 29 patients who were tested on only one hand, only 13 (45%) showed a normal performance for that hand.

2. The frequency of impaired tactile form perception is higher among patients with sensory or motor deficits than among those without such deficits. Among the 92 patients with unilateral lesions, those with sensory or motor impairment showed a 57% frequency of impairment as compared to a 44% frequency of impairment for those without sensory or motor deficits.

3. Bilateral (or ipsilateral) impairment in tactile form recognition is frequent in patients with unilateral lesions. Among the 64 patients who had both hands tested, 24 (38%) performed defectively with both hands. Among the 28 patients who had only one hand tested, 15 (54%) performed defectively with the hand ipsilateral to the side of lesion.

4. Nonaphasic patients with right hemisphere lesions show a higher frequency of impairment (59%) than do nonaphasic patients with left hemisphere lesions (38%). The frequency of impairment (58%) in aphasic patients with left hemisphere lesions is comparable to that of nonaphasic patients with right hemisphere lesions.

5. Nonaphasic patients with right hemisphere disease show a markedly higher frequency of bilateral or ipsilateral impairment (53%) than do nonaphasic patients with left hemisphere lesions (28%). The frequency of bilateral or ipsilateral impairment

TABLE 8-9   Tactile Form Perception: Performance Patterns in Patients with Brain Disease

Pattern	R.H. NoSMD n=23	R.H. SMD n=28	L.H. NA-NoSMD n=6	L.H. NA-SMD n=23	L.H. A-NoSMD n=7	L.H. A-SMD n=5	BIL n=12
A	11	3	5	7	4	1	2
B	1	–	–	–	–	–	1
C	5	8	–	2	–	–	5
D	–	–	1	–	2	1	–
E	4	1	–	–	–	–	–
F	1	1	–	3	1	–	1
G	1	1	–	–	–	–	2
AR	–	7	–	–	–	–	–
AL	–	–	–	6	–	–	–
BR	–	–	–	–	–	–	–
BL	–	–	–	1	–	1	–
(F)	–	7	–	–	–	–	1
(G)	–	–	–	4	–	2	–

R.H. NoSMD-Right hemisphere lesion, without sensory or motor defect.
R.H. SMD-Right hemisphere lesion, with sensory or motor defect.
L.H. NA-NoSMD-Left hemisphere lesion, not aphasic, without sensory or motor defect.
L.H. A-NoSMD-Left hemisphere lesion, aphasic, without sensory or motor defect.
L.H. NA-SMD-Left hemisphere lesion, not aphasic, with sensory or motor defect.
L.H. A-SMD-Left hemisphere lesion, aphasic, with sensory or motor defect.
BIL-Bilateral disease, nonaphasic, with or without sensory or motor defect.

(50%) in aphasic patients with left hemisphere lesions is comparable to that of nonaphasic patients with right hemisphere disease.

6. Patients with bilateral brain disease show a very high frequency of impairment (83%).

COMMENTS

A distinction between contralateral impairment and bilateral (or ipsilateral) impairment in tactile form perception should be made in considering the performances of patients with unilateral brain disease. It is reasonable to interpret contralateral impairment as a higher-level somesthetic defect related to injury of critical areas of the affected cerebral hemisphere and as being comparable in nature to other tactile-spatial defects such as loss of position sense and impaired recognition of the direction of lines drawn on the skin surface. But bilateral impairment, or unilateral impairment in the patient tested only on the hand ipsilateral to the side of the lesion, cannot be related in the same direct way to focal injury of the affected hemisphere.

The idea that patients with brain disease may manifest a generalized impairment in the capacity for spatial thought affecting all sensory modalities dates back to the late 19th century (cf. Benton, 1982). Empirical support for this idea has been provided by the studies of Corkin (1965), Dee and Benton (1970), De Renzi and Scotti (1969), Milner (1965), and Semmes (1965, 1968), all of which report significant associations between tactile-spatial and visuospatial performances in brain-injured patients. Dee and Benton (1970) found a particularly close relationship between failing performance with the ipsilateral hand on the tactile form perception test and visuoconstructive disability in patients with unilateral brain disease. It is quite possible that bilateral or ipsilateral failure in tactile form perception reflects a "supramodal" spatial disability rather than a specific somesthetic defect. Both this possibility and the basic question of the defining features of "supramodal" spatial disability deserve further study.

The patients with right hemisphere lesions showed a higher frequency of defective performance than did the nonaphasic patients with left hemisphere lesions. This finding is, of course, consistent with the concept that the right hemisphere plays a crucial role in mediating spatial performances in the somesthetic modality as well as in the visual and auditory modalities (cf. Benton, Levin & Varney, 1973; Benton, Varney & Hamsher, 1978). However, our small sample of aphasic patients with left hemisphere lesions showed as high a frequency of defect as did the patients with right hemisphere disease. Thus it appears that more than one neural mechanism is involved in the mediation of the performance.

As noted, a very high proportion of patients with bilateral disease performed defectively. While bilateral impairment was the most frequent type of failure, three patients showed unilateral defects—with the right hand in one case and with the left hand in two cases. It is possible that such an indication of specific unilateral defect would be useful in evaluating a patient with bilateral or "diffuse" disease.

REFERENCES

Benton A. L. (1982) Spatial thinking in neurological patients: historical aspects. In *Spatial Abilities: Development and Physiological Foundations*, M. Potegal (ed). New York: Academic Press.

Benton A. L., Levin H. S. & Varney N. R. (1973) Tactile perception of direction in normal subjects. *Neurology 23*: 1248–1250.

Benton A. L., Varney N. R. & Hamsher K. DeS. (1978) Lateral differences in tactile directional perception. *Neuropsychologia 16*: 109–114.

Corkin S. (1965) Tactually-guided maze learning in man: effects of unilateral cortical excisions and bilateral hippocampal lesions. *Neuropsychologia 3*: 339–351.

Dee H. L. & Benton A. L. (1970) A cross-modal investigation of spatial performances in patients with unilateral cerebral disease. *Cortex 6*: 261–272.

Delay J-P. L. (1935) *Les Astéréognosies: Pathologie du Toucher*. Paris: Masson.

De Renzi E. Scotti C. (1969) The influence of spatial disorders in impairing tactual discrimination of shapes. *Cortex 5*: 53–62.

Foerster O. (1901) Untersuchungen ueber das Localizationsvermoegen bei

Sensibilitaetsstoerungen: Ein Beitrag zur Psychophysiologie der Raumvorstellung. *Monatsschfrit fuer Psychiatrie und Neurologie 9*: 31–42.

Hoffmann H. (1885) Stereognostiche Versuche, angestellt zur Ermittelung der Elemente des Gefühlssinnes, aus denen die Vorstellungen der Körper im Raume gebildet werden. *Deutsches Archiv fuer Klinischen Medizin 36*: 398–426.

Milner B. (1965) Visually-guided maze learning in man: effects of bilateral hippocampal, bilateral frontal and unilateral cerebral lesions. *Neuropsychologia 3*: 317–338.

Semmes J. (1965) A non-tactual factor in stereognosis. *Neuropsychologia 3*: 295–315.

Semmes J. (1968) Hemispheric specialization: a possible clue to mechanism. *Neuropsychologia 6*: 11–26.

Spreen O. & Gaddes W. H. (1969) Developmental norms for 15 neuropsychological tests age 6 to 15 *Cortex 5*: 171–191.

Wernicke C. (1895) Zwei Fälle von Rindenläsion. *Arbeiten der Psychiatrischen Klinik in Breslau 2*: 33–53.

9. Finger Localization

BACKGROUND

Loss of the ability to name the fingers, to show them on verbal command, or to localize them after tactile stimulation first gained prominence as a symptom of brain disease in the 1920s when Gerstmann (1924, 1927, 1930) described patients who showed one or more of these deficits. He interpreted the performance failure as an expression of a limited disorder of the body schema. Coining the term "finger agnosia" for the disabilities, he ascribed their occurrence to focal disease in the territory of the angular gyrus of the left hemisphere. Later finger agnosia was made the nuclear symptom in the combination of deficits that came to be known as the Gerstmann syndrome and that included right–left disorientation, agraphia, and acalculia (Gerstmann, 1930, 1940).

Subsequently it became clear that finger recognition (and its pathological counterpart, finger agnosia) covered a range of specific performances which needed to be operationally defined. Schilder (1931) described five forms of defective finger recognition that could occur independently and asserted that each pointed to a different localization of the causative lesion. Benton (1959) classified finger recognition performances along a number of dimensions according to the nature of the stimulus (verbal or nonverbal, visual or tactile, single or multiple), the nature of the required response (verbal or nonverbal), and the extent of the impairment (bilateral or unilateral). Ettlinger's (1963) study of patients with finger agnosia disclosed a variety of performance patterns, e.g., some failed naming tasks but not nonverbal localization tasks, while others showed the opposite pattern.

The finger agnosia described by Gerstmann involved a bilateral impairment in recognition that extended to the fingers of the examiner as well as those of the patient's hands. However, Head (1920) had already described unilateral impairment in tactile finger localization as a form of sensory defect resulting from parietal lobe disease. It is obvious that this form of defective finger recognition is quite different in nature from the bilateral disturbances in naming and identifying by name to which Gerstmann called attention.

Thus it is apparent that an extensive battery of tests would be required to probe for the presence of all the disabilities that have been designated by the term "finger agnosia." Ettlinger employed a set of 12 tests for the purpose. Recent studies have tended to utilize test procedures that do not require the patient to name the fingers or to identify them by name; hence such procedures are applicable to aphasic as well as nonaphasic patients. Our own test is an example of such a "nonverbal" procedure.

DESCRIPTION

This 60-item test (Table 9-1) consists of three parts: (A) with the hand visible, localization of single fingers touched by the examiner with the pointed end of a pencil (10 trials on each hand); (B) with the hand hidden from view, localization of single fingers touched by the examiner (10 trials on each hand); (C) with the hand hidden from view, localization of pairs of fingers simultaneously touched by the examiner (10 trials each hand). The choice of mode of response is left up to the patient. He can name the touched fingers, point to them on an outline drawing of the stimulated hand, or call out their numbers (Fig. 9-1). The arrangement for localizing the fingers in the purely tactile tests (parts B and C) is shown in Figure 9-2.

In all parts of the test, the patient's hand rests on the table with the palms up and the fingers extended and slightly separated. In some patients with spastic hemiplegia the hand and fingers cannot be positioned to permit valid testing; assessment of finger recognition is restricted to the unaffected hand in these cases. (See Table 9-1.)

ADMINISTRATION

The test is introduced by saying, *"I am going to touch different fingers on your hand; you tell me which finger I touch. You can name the fingers, if you wish, or you can point to it on this card."* Proceed with Part A (tactile-visual stimulation) of the tests, touching the finger tips in the order indicated on the record sheet. The finger tip should be touched firmly with the pointed end of a pencil for about 2 seconds. There should be no question that the patient feels the stimulation. In patients with sensory defect or disturbed attention, the stimulation may be prolonged to 3–4 seconds to insure adequate reception of the stimulus. Some patients with severe sensory defect cannot be tested on the affected hand.

After completing Part A, say: *"Now put your (right, left) hand under this curtain. You won't see me touching your finger but you will feel it."* Guide the patient's hand, palm up, into the box; have him extend and slightly separate the fingers and insure that the posture is comfortable for him. *"Tell me which finger I touch. You can name the finger or point to it on this card or call the number of the card."* Proceed with Part B (tactile stimulation of single fingers) in the order indicated on the record sheet. However, it may not be possible to test both hands in a patient with a dense hemiplegia.

TABLE 9-1   Finger Localization: Record Form

Name _____ No. _____ Date _____

Age _____ Sex _____ Education _____ Handedness _____ Examiner _____

Finger localization (Form B)*

A. Identification of Single Fingers—Hand Visible

Tips of fingers are touched in the following order (1 = thumb; 5 = little finger):

Score
R___
L___
         Right Hand 2__5__3__1__4__3__5__2__4__1__
         Left Hand 1__4__2__5__3__4__1__3__5__2__

B. Identification of Single Fingers—Hand Hidden

Tips of fingers are touched in the following order:

Score
R___
L___
         Right Hand 5__1__3__2__4__3__5__1__4__2__
         Left Hand 2__4__1__5__3__4__2__3__1__5__

C. Identification of Two Simultaneously Touched Fingers—Hand Hidden

Score
R___
L___
         Right Hand 1-4__2-3__2-4__3-5__3-4__2-3__2-5__1-2__3-4__1-3__
         Left Hand 1-3__3-4__1-2__2-5__2-3__3-4__3-5__2-4__2-3__1-4__

Total Score _____   R Score _____   L Score _____

*Form A consists of the identical sequences of trials with the difference that the right hand sequences are presented to the left hand and vice versa.

After completion of Part B, say: *"Now I am going to touch two of your fingers at the same time. Tell me which fingers I touch. Again, either name the fingers or point to them on the card or call their numbers on the card."*

RECORDING AND SCORING

Correct responses may be checked but incorrect responses should be recorded by number. Responses on Part C are counted as correct only if both fingers are accurately identified. As indicated on the record sheet, a total score for the whole test and separate scores for the right and left hands are computed.

NORMATIVE OBSERVATIONS

The test was given to 104 hospitalized control patients (64 men, 40 women) without history or evidence of brain disease or psychiatric illness. The samples ranged in age from 16 to 65 years and in educational level from 5 to 16+ years. Thirty-one patients made perfect scores of 60 on the test and an additional 31

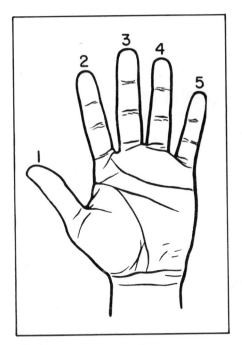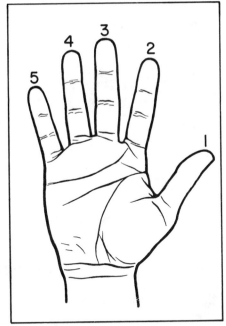

Fig. 9-1 Outline drawings of the right and left hands on which subject identifies stimulated fingers by pointing to them or calling their number.

patients made scores of 58–59. Thus 60% of the group made 2 errors or less. The mean score was 57.5 (SD = 2.7). No difference between the mean score of the men (57.4, SD = 2.7) and that of the women (57.7, SD = 2.6) was apparent.

The relationship of age and educational level to performance was assessed by comparing subgroups of patients as shown in Table 9-2. There was no indication that either age (within the 16–65 years limit) or education influenced performance levels, and hence no score corrections were necessary. The distribution of total scores in the sample is shown in Table 9-3.

Single-Hand Performances   Since unilateral as well as bilateral impairment in finger localization may occur, separate normative values for each hand were computed. Table 9-4 shows the distributions of scores for the right and the left hand in the control group. As will be seen, the distributions are very similar. The mean scores for the right and left hands were 28.65 and 28.84, respectively.

The distribution of the differences in score between the right and left hands was also computed in order to provide a normative basis for interpreting asymmetry in performance level in the individual patient. Table 9-5 shows this distribution. A difference in score of two points or less was shown by 94% of the control patients. An additional four patients showed score differences of three to four points. Only two patients showed score differences of five to six points.

As would be expected, most of the errors were made on Part C of the test

Fig. 9-2 Arrangement for finger localization without the aid of vision.

(localization of simultaneously touched fingers). Of the total number of 258 errors made by the 104 patients, 211 (82%) were on Part C. Table 9-6 shows the distribution of error scores for each hand in the three parts of the test. Errors in Part A (tactile-visual localization of single fingers) were extremely rare; only six errors were made in 2080 trials for an error rate of 0.3%. The error rate on Part B (tactile localization of single fingers) was 2.0% with an occasional patient making two errors on one or the other hand. In contrast, the error rate in Part C was 10.1% with some patients making four to six errors on one or the other hand.

A number of performance patterns have been defined on the basis of these normative data.

   A. *Normal*. Total score = 51–60, single-hand scores = 25–30, right–left difference of 0–3 points.
   B. *Borderline*. Total score = 49–51; one single-hand score = 23–24 and one single hand score = 26–27, right–left difference = 0–3 points.
   C. *Bilateral symmetric defect*. Single-hand scores = less than 26, right–left difference = 0–3 points.

D. *Bilateral asymmetric (right hand) defect.* Single-hand scores = less than 26; right-hand score 4 or more points lower than left-hand score.

E. *Bilateral asymmetric (left hand) defect.* Single-hand scores = less than 26; left-hand score 4 or more points less than right hand score.

F. *Right unilateral defect.* Right-hand score 4 or more points less than left-hand score of 26 or higher.

G. *Left unilateral defect.* Left-hand score 4 or more points less than right-hand score of 26 or higher.

AR. *Normal right hand.* Right-hand score = 26–30; left hand not tested.

AL. *Normal left hand.* Left-hand score = 26–30; right hand not tested.

BR. *Borderline right.* Right-hand score = 25; left hand not tested.

BL. *Borderline left.* Left-hand score = 25; right hand not tested.

(F) *Right-hand defect.* Right-hand score less than 25; left hand not tested.

(G) *Left-hand defect.* Left-hand score less than 25; right hand not tested.

PERFORMANCES OF CHILDREN

Visual discrimination of the fingers begins to develop during the third and fourth years of life. As Table 9-7, which is derived from the data of Lefford, Birch, and Green (1974), indicates, about 75% of 3-year-old children and all but a few 4-year-old children are able to point to a finger which they have seen the examiner touch or point to. Tactile discrimination of the fingers develops more slowly. When deprived of vision, only about 25% of 3-year-olds and about 60% of 4-year-olds can point to a finger touched by the examiner. Localization of a touched finger on a model of the hand is an even more difficult task for children of preschool age. Only about 10% of 3-year-olds, 30% of 4-year-olds, and 50% of 5-year-olds succeed on this task. Thus our test, which requires either naming touched fingers or pointing to them on a model of the hand, is too difficult for many preschool children. As will be seen, this capacity develops throughout the school years.

The original version of our test differed from the final version in that Part C (tactile localization of simultaneously touched fingers) consisted of five trials on each hand instead of ten. The original version was used in developing normative standards of performance in school children (Benton, 1955a, 1959; Wake, 1956, 1957). In order to make the findings for children directly comparable to those for adults, the children's scores have been prorated by doubling the number correct score on Part C for each hand before computing the total score.

The normative observations to be presented are based on the performances of 204 children from the studies of Benton (1955a, 1959) and 612 children from the studies of Wake (1956, 1957), all of whom were in the age range of 6 to 12 years. One sample of 158 children in the Benton studies had WISC Verbal Scale IQs within the range of 85–115. A second sample of 46 children of superior intelligence had WISC Verbal Scale IQs ranging from 116 to 138. Intelligence level was not controlled in Wake's studies. One part of the sample consisted of randomly selected children at the Hull Protestant School near Ottawa who appeared to be of

TABLE 9-2   Finger Localization: Mean Scores in Relation to Age and Educational Background

Education, yrs.		Age, yrs.		
		16–45	46–55	56–65
13+	M	57	57	–
	SD	2.3	–	–
	n	7	1	0
12	M	58	58	–
	SD	2.6	2.0	–
	n	24	8	0
8–11	M	58	57	58
	SD	2.8	3.5	1.6
	n	28	16	8
5–7	M	60	56	57
	SD	–	3.0	1.7
	n	1	7	4

TABLE 9-3   Finger Localization: Distribution of Scores

Score	n	Percentile rank	Classification
60	31	85+	
59	15	70th	
58	16	56th	
57	13	40th	Normal
56	12	28th	
55	5	16th	
54	5	12th	
53	1	7th	
52	0	7th	Borderline
51	1	6th	
50	3	5th	
49	1	2nd	Moderately defective
48	1	1st	
0–47	0	0	Severely defective
	104		

TABLE 9-4   Finger Localization: Distributions of Scores in Right and Left Hands

Score	Right hand *n*	Percentile rank	Left hand *n*	Percentile rank	Classification
30	38	82+	45	78+	
29	28	63	29	57	Normal
28	18	37	16	29	
27	12	19	7	13	
26	4	8	3	7	Borderline
25	2	4	2	4	
24	–	–	–	–	Moderately defective
23	2	2	–	–	
22	–		2	2	
<22	–		–		Severely defective

TABLE 9-5   Finger Localization: Distribution of Differences Between Right and Left-Hand Scores

Absolute difference	*n*	Right hand higher score	Left hand higher score	Percentile rank	Classification
0	50	–	–	–	
1	33	14	19	52	Normal
2	15	3	12	20	
3	2	0	2	6	Borderline
4	2	2	0	4	
5	1	0	1	2	Moderate dissociation
6	1	1	0	1	
7+	–	–	–	–	Extreme dissociation

TABLE 9-6   Finger Localization: Distribution of Error Scores in Parts A, B, and C

Number of errors	Part A RH	LH	Part B RH	LH	Part C RH	LH
0	102	102	84	89	46	47
1	2	1	17	12	27	31
2	–	0	3	3	18	15
3		1	–	–	7	9
4		–			3	1
5					1	0
6					2	1
7					–	–

TABLE 9-7   Finger Localization: Performances of Preschool Children*

Task	Percentage performing task, age		
	3 yrs.	4 yrs.	5 yrs.
Visual-tactile localization on self	73%	93%	99%
Tactile localization on self	24	63	72
Visual–tactile localization on model	15	45	82
Tactile localization on model	11	28	52

*Data from Lefford, Birch & Green (1974).

TABLE 9-8   Finger Localization: Performances of School Children

Age	Benton[1] average children		Wake[2]		Benton[1] superior children	
	(n)	mean score	(n)	mean score	(n)	mean score
6	(40)	38.6	(120)	41.8	(8)	44.5
7	(41)	44.4	(62)	46.1	(8)	48.3
8	(38)	48.1	(52)	49.8	(15)	49.8
9	(39)	50.9	(74)	51.7	(15)	52.2
10			(108)	53.0		
11			(126)	53.8		
12			(70)	54.4		

[1] Data from Benton (1955a, 1959).
[2] Data from Wake (1956, 1957).

TABLE 9-9   Finger Localization: Mean Scores of Children on Parts A, B, and C ($n=158$)

Age	Total score	Part A[1]	Part B[2]	Part C[3]
6 yrs.	38.6	17.7	13.5	7.4
7	44.4	19.3	16.5	8.6
8	48.1	19.6	17.5	11.0
9	50.9	19.8	18.6	12.5

[1] Visual–tactile localization of single fingers.
[2] Tactile localization of single fingers.
[3] Tactile localization of simultaneously touched pairs of fingers.

average socioeconomic and intellectual status. The other part consisted of children recruited from among relatives and friends and these may have come from an above-average socioeconomic background.

The mean scores for ages 6 through 12 are shown in Table 9-8. As will be seen, there is a progressive rise in performance level through the age of 12 years. The mean scores of the Canadian sample are consistently higher than those of the Iowa sample of children of average intelligence. It seems likely that the difference is attributable to the inclusion of children of superior intelligence in the Canadian sample. As the table indicates, the sample of children with superior intelligence performed at a higher level than did the children in either of the larger groups. It also appears that the adult level of performance has not been reached at the age of 12 years.

Table 9-9 shows the scores on Parts A, B, and C of the battery made by the 158 children of average intelligence in the Benton studies. As will be seen, 6-year-olds find the tactile localization of single fingers to be a difficult task and it is only at age 9 that relatively few errors are made on it. Nine-year-olds experience considerable difficulty in the tactile localization of simultaneously touched pairs of fingers. Their high error rate of 37.5% on Part C (roughly four times as high as that of adults) accounts in large part for their relatively low total scores.

PERFORMANCES OF PATIENTS WITH BRAIN DISEASE

The test findings in 61 right-handed patients with brain disease are summarized in Table 9-10. The sample was composed of patients in the following diagnostic categories:

1. Bilateral disease (20 cases); predominantly diffuse degenerative disease; a few with bilateral focal lesions (e.g., metastatic carcinoma).
2. Right hemisphere disease (19 cases); predominantly vascular disease; no patient was aphasic.
3. Left hemisphere (22 cases); predominantly vascular disease.
   A. Nonaphasic (15 cases)
   B. Aphasic (7 cases)

The age range in this sample was 18–64. All the patients were tested on both hands.

Inspection of Table 9-10, which presents the results in terms of the defined performance patterns, indicates that:

1. The overall frequency of abnormal performances of diverse types (Patterns B to F) was very high. Only 26 (43%) of the 61 patients achieved a normal performance.
2. The overall frequency of abnormal performance was higher in the nonaphasic patients with bilateral disease (70%) and the aphasic patients (86%) than in the nonaphasic patients with unilateral disease (42–47%).
3. Bilateral impairment in finger localization (Patterns C and D) was quite common in

TABLE 9-10 Finger Localization: Performance Patterns in Patients with Brain Disease

Patterns*	Diagnostic category			
	Bilateral (*n*=20)	Right (*n*=19)	Left Nonaphasic (*n*=15)	Left aphasic (*n*=7)
A. Normal	6 (30%)	11 (58%)	8 (53%)	1 (14%)
B. Borderline	2 (10%)	2 (10.5%)	–	–
C. Bilateral symmetric	11 (55%)	2 (10.5%)	–	4 (57%)
D. Bilateral asymmetric (R)	–	–	2 (13.3%)	–
E. Bilateral asymmetric (L)	–	–	–	–
F. Right unilateral	1 (5%)	–	5 (33.3%)	2 (29%)
G. Left unilateral	–	4 (21%)	–	–

*See text for definitions of patterns.

  the patients with bilateral disease (55%) and the aphasic patients (57%). In contrast, only a small proportion of the nonaphasic patients with unilateral disease showed bilateral impairment (11–13%).

4. Unilateral defect on the side opposite to the side of lesion was the most common abnormal performance pattern (21–33%) in nonaphasic patients with unilateral disease.

Gainotti, Cianchetti, and Tiacci (1972) found that when the test was given to large samples of right-handed patients with unilateral disease, the frequency of bilateral impairment (Patterns C, D, E) was contingent upon whether or not the patient was aphasic and/or mentally deteriorated. Their results, which are shown in Table 9-11, indicate clearly that it is quite uncommon for a unilaterally damaged patient who is not aphasic or suffering from general mental impairment to show bilateral defects in finger localization. In a second study, Gainotti and Tiacci (1973) investigated *unilateral* impairment and found that contralateral impairment was shown with significantly higher frequency by patients with right hemisphere lesions (*n*=77) as compared to those with left lesions (*n*=99). As Table 9-10 shows, we did not find this difference in our small series. Gainotti and Tiacci also observed that some patients without evident somatosensory defect, as indexed by normal responses to double simultaneous tactile stimulation, nevertheless showed defective unilateral finger localization.

  Table 9-12 shows the distribution of error scores for each hand on Parts A, B, and C of the test in 20 randomly selected patients with brain disease. Comparison with the performances of control patients (Table 9-5) indicates that Parts B and C (tactile localization) provide the basis for the discrimination between the two diagnostic groups. Part A (visual-tactile localization) is relatively non-discriminative, with only two of the 20 patients making more than one error on a single hand.

TABLE 9-11   Finger Localization: Bilateral Impairment in Patients with Unilateral Lesions*

Left hemisphere lesions (*n*=88)	16 (18%)
Mentally deteriorated (*n*=30)	10 (33%)
Not mentally deteriorated (*n*=58)	6 (10%)
Aphasic (*n*=34)	13 (38%)
Not aphasic (*n*=54)	3 (6%)
Right hemisphere lesions (*n*=74)	12 (16%)
Mentally deteriorated (*n*=22)	10 (45%)
Not mentally deteriorated (*n*=52)	2 (4%)

*Adapted from Gainotti, Cianchetti & Tiacci (1972).

COMMENTS

The necessity for making a sharp distinction between bilateral and unilateral defects in finger localization is obvious. Gerstmann's bilateral "finger agnosia" and Head's unilateral impairment in the tactile localization of the fingers are two quite different conditions, each with its own correlates and diagnostic implications. Thus the total score on a finger localization test without consideration of performance levels on the different components of the test may lead to faulty conclusions.

Bilateral impairment in finger localization is closely associated with both aphasic disorder and general mental impairment (Benton, 1959, 1962; Poeck & Orgass, 1969; Sauguet, Benton & Hécaen, 1971; Gainotti, Cianchetti & Tiacci, 1972). Yet many aphasics and demented patients show intact finger localization capacity and the question of whether bilateral finger agnosia has distinctive significance for lesional localization is still unresolved.

Impaired finger localization is encountered among deviant children in different diagnostic categories. Some mentally retarded patients show grossly defective performances, far below the level that would be predicted from their mental age (Strauss & Werner, 1938; Benton, 1955b, 1959). Clawson (1962) gave our finger localization test to small samples of brain-injured, emotionally disturbed and normal children who had been matched for age (range = 8–13 years) and WISC IQ (range = 91–123). She found that 80% of the brain-injured children performed at a level exceeded by 90% of the normal and emotionally disturbed children.

The relationship between finger localization and reading achievement in children has been the topic of much research. The findings with respect to a *concurrent* association between defective finger localization and specific reading disability have been inconsistent (cf. Benton, 1979). At best, the association is a tenuous one and it is more likely to be found in younger children in the early

TABLE 9-12 Finger Localization: Distribution of Error Scores in Brain-Diseased Patients (*n*=20)

Number of errors	Part A		Part B		Part C	
	RH	LH	RH	LH	RH	LH
0	17	18	10	9	–	–
1	1	1	3	4	3	2
2	1	–	1	1	1	5
3	–	–	2	–	2	2
4	–	–	–	1	5	2
5	–	–	–	2	3	2
6	1	1	3	–	1	2
7	–	–	1	1	2	2
8	–	–	–	1	–	2
9	–	–	–	–	3	–
10	–	–	–	1	–	1

school grades than among older children. On the other hand, there is evidence that the performances of kindergarten children on finger localization tests is a significant *predictor* of subsequent reading achievement (Fletcher, Taylor, Morris & Satz, 1982; Lindgren, 1978; Satz & Friel, 1973, 1974; Satz, Taylor, Friel & Fletcher, 1978). Why finger localization performances should have this predictive significance remains unclear.

REFERENCES

Benton A. L. (1955a) Development of finger localization capacity in school children. *Child Development 26*: 225–230.

Benton A. L. (1955b) Right-left discrimination and finger localization in defective children. *Arch. Neurol. Psychiat. 74*: 583–589.

Benton A. L. (1959) *Right-Left Discrimination and Finger Localization: Development and Pathology.* New York: Hoeber-Harper.

Benton A. L. (1962) Clinical symptomatology in right and left hemisphere lesions. In *Interhemispheric Relations and Cerebral Dominance*, V. B. Montcastle (ed). Baltimore: Johns Hopkins Press.

Benton A. L. (1977) Reflections on the Gerstmann syndrome. *Brian and Language 4*: 45–62.

Benton A. L. (1979) The neuropsychological significance of finger recognition. In *Cognitive Growth and Development*, M. Bortner (ed). New York: Brunner/Mazel.

Clawson A. (1962) Relationship of psychological tests to cerebral disorders in children. *Psychol. Rep. 10*: 187–190.

Ettlinger G. E. (1963) Defective identification of fingers. *Neuropsychologia 1*: 39–45.

Fletcher J. M., Taylor H. G., Morris R. & Satz P. (1982) Finger recognition skills and reading achievement: a developmental neuropsychological perspective. *Dev. Psychol. 18*: 124–132.

Gainotti G., Cianchetti C. & Tiacci, C. (1972) The influence of hemispheric side of lesions on non-verbal tasks of finger localization. *Cortex 8*: 364–381.

Gainotti G. & Tiacci C. (1973) The unilateral forms of finger agnosia. *Confinia Neurologica 35*: 271–284.

Gerstmann J. (1924) Fingeragnosie: eine umschriebene Störung der Orientierung am eigenen Körper. *Wien. klin. Wchnschr. 37*: 1010–1012.

Gerstmann J. (1927) Fingeragnosie und isolierte Agraphie: ein neues Syndrom. *Ztschr. Neurol. Psychiat. 108*: 152–177.

Gerstmann J. (1930) Zir Symptomatologie der Hirnläsionen im Uebergangsgebiet der unteren Parietal- und mittleren Occipitalwindung. *Nervenarzt 3*: 691–695.

Gerstmann J. (1940) Syndrome of finger agnosia, disorientation for right and left, agraphia and acalculia. *Arch. Neurol. Psychiat. 44*: 398–408.

Head H. (1920) *Studies in Neurology*. London: Oxford University Press.

Lefford A., Birch H. G. & Green G. (1974) The perceptual and cognitive bases for finger localization and selective finger movement in preschool children. *Child Development 45*: 335–343.

Lindgren S. D. (1978) Finger localization and the prediction of reading disability. *Cortex 14*: 87–101.

Poeck K. & Orgass B. (1969) An experimental investigation of finger agnosia. *Neurology 19*: 801–807.

Satz P. & Friel J. (1973) Some predictive antecedents of specific learning disability. In *The Disabled Learner*, P. Satz & J. Ross (eds). Rotterdam: Rotterdam University Press.

Satz P. & Friel, J. (1974) Some predictive antecedents of specific reading disability: a preliminary two-year follow-up. *J. Learning Dis. 7*: 437–444.

Satz P., Taylor H. G., Friel J. & Fletcher J. (1978) Some developmental and predictive precursors of reading disabilities: a six-year follow-up. In *Dyslexia*, A. L. Benton & D. Pearl (eds). New York: Oxford University Press.

Sauguet J., Benton A. L. & Hécaen H. (1971) Disturbances of the body schema in relation to language impairment and hemispheric locus of lesion. *J. Neurol. Neurosurg. Psychiat. 34*: 496–501.

Schilder P. (1931) Fingeragnosie, Fingerapraxie, Fingeraphasie. *Nervenarzt 4*: 625–629.

Strauss A. & Werner H. (1938) Deficiency in the finger schema in relation to arithmetic disability. *Am. J. Orthopsychiat. 8*: 719–725.

Wake F. R. (1956) Finger localization in Canadian school children. Presented at Annual Meeting of Canadian Psychological Association, Ottawa, June 1956.

Wake, F. R. (1957) Finger localization scores in defective children. Presented in Annual Meeting of Canadian Psychological Association, Toronto, June 1957.

10. Phoneme Discrimination

BACKGROUND

From the beginning of the modern study of aphasic disorders it was appreciated that the failure of a patient to understand a spoken statement or command could be caused by one or more of a number of factors, such as impaired auditory discrimination of sounds in general or the particular sounds represented by phonemes, inability to achieve an accurate perception of sequences of sound, defective grasp of the syntactic structure of a message, or faulty apprehension of its semantic import.

In line with this thinking, Kleist (1962) classified disorders of oral verbal comprehension into two broad categories, "speech sound deafness" (*Sprachklangtaubheit*) and "speech sense deafness" (*Sprachsinntaubheit*). Similarly, both Hécaen (1969) and Luria (1970) hypothesized that the defects in oral verbal comprehension shown by some aphasic patients result from a specific disturbance in "phonemic decoding" or "complex auditory discrimination" that prevents adequate perception of the speech sounds. In other cases, the impairment in oral verbal comprehension is due to difficulty in apprehending sequences of speech sounds or failure to associate meaning with the speech percept.

A number of studies (Basso, Casati & Vignolo, 1977; Blumstein, Baker & Goodglass, 1977; Tallal & Newcombe, 1978; Varney & Benton, 1979; Miceli, Gainotti, Caltagirone & Masullo, 1980) have investigated the relationship of accuracy in phoneme discrimination to the level of oral language comprehension in aphasic patients. The findings of these studies will be considered in the discussion section.

DESCRIPTION

The test, which is designed to be a brief screening instrument, consists of 30 tape-recorded pairs of nonsense words spoken by an adult male (Table 10-1). Ten pairs consist of one-syllable words and 20 pairs of two-syllable words. In 15 test items,

TABLE 10-1 Phoneme Discrimination Record Form*

Name ———————————————————— No. ——————— Date ————————————

Age ————— Sex ————— Education ————— Handedness ————— Examiner ————

Item	Response	Item	Response
1. (D) bä-bō	————	16. (D) gḗtä-gätä	————
2. (D) sē-sōō	————	17. (S) arak-arak	————
3. (S) tō-tō	————	18. (D) aksäd-aksän	————
4. (D) ur-är	————	19. (D) vemḗ-venḗ	————
5. (S) bä-bä	————	20. (S) kejḗ-kejḗ	————
6. (S) lōō-lōō	————	21. (S) pedzap-pedzap	————
7. (D) nō-tō	————	22. (D) kwēfäb-kwēfäd	————
8. (S) ur-ur	————	23. (D) ûrsit-ûrsat	————
9. (S) sōō-sōō	————	24. (S) slidig-slidig	————
10. (D) dōō-lōō	————	25. (D) pedzap-pelzap	————
11. (S) vemḗ-vemḗ	————	26. (D) lamäd-lēmäd	————
12. (S) aksän-aksän	————	27. (S) kwēfäd-kwēfäd	————
13. (D) kejḗ-kejō	————	28. (D) klidig-slidig	————
14. (S) gätä-gätä	————	29. (S) ûrsat-ûrsat	————
15. (D) ōrak-ôrak	————	30. (S) lamäd-lamäd	————

No. correct *Same* responses ————   No. *Same* errors ————

No. correct *Different* responses————   No. *Different* errors ————

　　　　　　　Total Correct ————   Total Errors ————

Comments:

*The sound symbols are those of the pronunciation key of the *Random House Dictionary of the English Language* (New York, 1967).*

the word pairs differ in one phonemic feature, with the target stimuli primarily involving vowels and liquid consonants. With one exception, each word appearing in a "same" pair also appears in a "different" pair. On each block of ten trials, five items are the same and five are different. The items represent only a small fraction of the possible phonemic contrasts and cannot be utilized to identify qualitative characteristics of performance, e.g., whether more errors are made on consonants than on vowels or on voicing contrasts than on place contrasts (cf. Blumstein, 1981).

ADMINISTRATION

The test should be given in a quiet room through a cassette tape recorder with less than 5% distortion and minimal background noise. Many commercially available cassette tape recorders meet these criteria but most dictaphones do not. Loudness may be adjusted to meet the individual patient's requirements.

Before beginning the test, insure that the patient understands the nature of the task and the required response. If there is any doubt about this point, a series of pairs of objects should be presented to him with the instruction: *"Are these the same or different?"* The series that we have generally used is as follows: *pen and paper; paper and paper; paper and book; pen and pen; book and book.* At this time, the patient's manner of response should be determined. If he is clearly capable of making a vocal response, he should be instructed to say *same* or *different.* If the possibility or validity of a vocal response is doubtful and if the patient can read, large-type printed cards with the words *same* and *different* can be presented for him to point to. If, as will often be the case, neither a reliable vocalization nor reading response is possible, the patient should be instructed to indicate by nodding or gesture whether the sounds in the pair are the same or different.

It is not uncommon to encounter confusion or a response set (always answering *same* or *different*) among aphasic patients. The phoneme discrimination should be given only to patients who are capable of producing reliable same–different responses to these pairs of objects.

SCORING

Credit one point for each correct response on the 30 test items. Since there are only two response alternatives on each test trial, a chance level of performance is 50% correct. Thus, the effective range of scores is 30 to 15 correct.

Tally the errors on *same* and *different* items separately (see Table 10-1). If most of the errors occur on *same* items, it is possible that the performance is invalid, and that the patient was attending to nonrelevant features of the stimuli. Also note whether more than 20 errors are made. These performances are significantly poorer than would be expected on a chance basis and probably reflect confusion about the required same–different responses.

NORMATIVE OBSERVATIONS

The distribution of scores of 30 hospitalized patients without history or evidence of brain disease, psychiatric illness, or hearing loss is shown in Table 10-2. No patient was over the age of 65 years. As will be seen, the great majority made scores of 25 or higher. Three patients (10%) made scores of 22–24. On the basis of these limited data, a score of less than 22 was classified as defective.

PERFORMANCES OF PATIENTS WITH BRAIN DISEASE

The distribution of scores in a sample of 16 nonaphasic right-handed patients with lesions of the right hemisphere is also shown in Table 10-2. As will be seen, 15

TABLE 10-2 Phoneme Discrimination: Distributions of Scores

Score	Controls (n=30)	Nonaphasic right B.D. (n=16)	Aphasic left B.D. (n=100)	Controls, live-voice (n=89)
30	3	1	5	51
29	5	2	6	17
28	8	3	12	13
27	6	3	16	3
26	3	2	10	2
25	2	2	9	2
24	1	1	7	–
23	1	–	5	–
22	1	1	6	1
21		1	3	
20			3	
19			1	
18			2	
17			2	
16			5	
15			5	
14			2	
13			1	

patients performed within normal limits and one patient made a score of 21, i.e., one point below the cut-off score.

The scores of 100 aphasic patients with left hemisphere lesions are also shown in Table 10-2. Of these, 24 made defective scores ranging from 13 to 21 correct. The scores of 17 patients (i.e., 13–18 correct) were at or near the chance level of success and may be regarded as reflecting grossly defective performances. The performances of the remaining seven patients with scores of 19–21 may be classified as moderately defective.

The relationship between level of phoneme discrimination and oral verbal understanding is shown in Table 10-3. As will be seen, none of the 17 patients with severely impaired phoneme discrimination showed intact oral verbal understanding. Of the seven patients with moderately impaired phoneme discrimination, two showed intact oral verbal understanding. At the same time, many patients with intact capacity for phoneme discrimination were impaired in oral verbal understanding.

COMMENT

It would seem obvious that impairment of phoneme discrimination necessarily entails a corresponding impairment of oral verbal understanding in aphasic patients. Yet the role of defective phonemic perception as a determinant of

TABLE 10-3   Phoneme Discrimination: Performances of Aphasic Patients with Intact and Defective Oral Verbal Comprehension

Phoneme discrimination score	Oral comprehension	
	Intact (*n*=42)	Defective* (*n*=58)
30–29	6	5
28–27	13	15
26–25	10	9
24–23	8	4
22	3	3
21	1	2
20	1	2
19	–	1
18	–	2
17	–	2
16	–	5
15	–	5
14	–	2
13	–	1

*Defective comprehension was defined as a score below that of 95% of control patients on the Aural Comprehension Test of the Multilingual Aphasia Examination (Benton & Hamsher, 1977).

defective comprehension of spoken language has been a controversial question.

Our results confirm those of two earlier studies in finding that there is a significant association between the phonological and semantic levels of auditory information processing and suggesting that, as Hécaen (1969) and Luria (1970) postulated, the impairment in oral verbal comprehension of some aphasic patients may be based primarily on a failure in phoneme discrimination. Tallal and Newcombe (1978) gave a series of audioperceptual tests to ten subjects with mild or moderate aphasic disorder as well as to ten nonaphasic subjects with right hemisphere lesions and six control subjects. Oral verbal comprehension was measured by the Token Test (De Renzi & Vignolo, 1962). Seven of the ten aphasic subjects performed defectively on a task requiring the discrimination between consonant–vowel syllables (e.g., *ba* vs. *da*) and six of these seven subjects also performed defectively on the Token Test. Varney and Benton (1979) assessed the relationship between phonemic discrimination, as assessed by our test (Table 10-2), and oral verbal comprehension, as assessed by the aural comprehension test of the Multilingual Aphasia Examination (Benton & Hamsher, 1977) in 39 aphasic patients. Ten patients (26%) performed defectively in phoneme discrimination and all showed impairment in oral verbal comprehension. Among the 29 patients with adequate phoneme comprehension, 13 (45%) showed intact oral verbal comprehension and 16 (55%) showed defective oral verbal comprehension. The findings of both studies, as well as the data presented above, indicate that intact phonemic discrimination is a necessary but not a sufficient basis for intact oral verbal comprehension in aphasic patients.

However, other studies have reported less clear results. Blumstein, Baker, and Goodglass (1977) investigated the relationship between the ability of aphasic patients to discriminate phonological contrasts and their level of oral verbal comprehension, as assessed by subtests of the Boston Diagnostic Aphasia Battery (Goodglass & Kaplan, 1972). A product-moment coefficient of .58 between performance level on the phonological tests and level of oral verbal comprehension was found, a statistic comparable to the rank-order correlation coefficient of .61 found by Varney and Benton. But the Wernicke patients in the sample, who showed more severe impairment in oral verbal comprehension than did the nonfluent aphasics, were superior to the nonfluent aphasics in the phonological tasks. Hence it was concluded that the comprehension deficit of the Wernicke aphasics could not be attributed to a deficit in phonemic discrimination.

The findings of Basso, Casati, and Vignolo (1977) led to a similar conclusion. In this study, aphasic and nonaphasic patients were required to identify the boundary zone between voiced and voiceless consonants. While nonaphasic patients with lesions in either hemisphere performed at a normal level, as defined by the performances of control patients, 74% of the aphasic patients performed defectively. Moreover, a systematic relationship between the severity of the phonemic identification defects and Token Test score was evident. However, since some patients who were markedly defective in phoneme discrimination showed only moderately impaired oral verbal comprehension, it was concluded that defects in phonemic identification were not "crucially" associated with level of oral verbal comprehension.

Still another study yielding equivocal results was that of Miceli, Gainotti, Caltagirone, and Masullo (1980). Again, a positive relationship between phonemic discrimination and performance level on tests of oral verbal comprehension was found. However, a substantial number of patients with inferior performances on the phonemic discrimination test achieved satisfactory scores on the comprehension tests.

The contradictory implications of the several studies on the question of the relationship between phonemic discrimination and oral verbal comprehension remain unresolved. That an aphasic patient may fail to understand meaningful speech messages within the context of intact capacity for phonemic discrimination is easy to understand. The reverse situation in which a patient understands the message despite impairment in phonemic discrimination calls for explanation. Miceli and colleagues suggest that such factors as contextual clues, as well as acoustic and semantic constraints, may facilitate comprehension of a meaningful message within the setting of impairment in phonemic discrimination.

Live-Voice Presentation   Some data on the performances of control patients without history or evidence of brain disease when the syllables were uttered by the same male examiner within the patient's view have been collected. The distribution of the scores of 89 patients is shown in Table 10-2. As would be expected, the live-voice presentation proved to be an easier task than the standard tape-recorded presentation. Seventy-six percent of the patients made perfect or near-perfect performances (scores of 29–30) with the live-voice presentation, as compared to 27% with the tape presentation. Conversely, only one patient (1%) made a score of less than 25 with the live-voice presentation, as compared to 10% with the tape presentation.

No doubt the opportunity to see the examiner's speech movements as he utters the syllables and the elimination of acoustic distortion associated with tape recording are the major factors responsible for the superior performance under the live-voice condition. Although, of course, the tape presentation provides a purer test of phoneme discrimination, the findings obtained with a live-voice (or videotape) presentation may prove useful for clinical or investigative purposes. For example, it would be of interest to determine whether or not the relatively few patients who showed good oral verbal comprehension (live-voice condition) despite defective phoneme discrimination (tape condition) also show improvement in phonemic discrimination under a live-voice condition.

REFERENCES

Basso A., Casati G. & Vignolo L. A. (1977) Phonemic identification defect in aphasia. *Cortex 13*: 85–95.

Benton A. L. & Hamsher K. (1977) *Multilingual Aphasia Examination.* Iowa City, Iowa: University of Iowa.

Blumstein S. (1981) Phonological aspects of aphasia. In *Acquired Aphasia*, M. T. Sarno (ed). New York: Academic Press.

Blumstein S. E., Baker E. & Goodglass H. (1977) Phonological factors in auditory comprehension in aphasia. *Neuropsychologia 15*: 19–30.

De Renzi E. & Vignolo L. (1962) The Token test: a sensitive test to detect receptive disturbances in aphasia. *Brain 85*: 665–678.

Goodglass H. & Kaplan E. (1972) *The Assessment of Aphasia and Related Disorders.* Philadelphia: Lea and Febiger.

Hécaen H. (1969) Essai de dissociation du syndrome de l'aphasie sensorielle. *Rev. Neurol. 120*: 229–237.

Kleist K. (1962) *Sensory Aphasia and Amusia.* Oxford: Pergamon Press.

Luria A. R. (1970) *Traumatic Aphasia.* The Hague: Mouton.

Miceli G., Gainotti G., Caltagirone C. & Masullo C. (1980) Some aspects of phonological impairment in aphasia. *Brain and Language 11*: 159–169.

Tallal P. & Newcombe F. (1978) Impairment of auditory perception and language comprehension in dysphasia. *Brain and Language 6*: 13–24.

Varney N. R. & Benton A. L. (1979) Phonemic discrimination and aural comprehension among aphasic patients. *J. Clin. Neuropsych. 1*: 65–73.

11. Three-Dimensional Block Construction

BACKGROUND

The concept of "constructional apraxia" was introduced into clinical neurology by Kleist (1923, 1934; Strauss, 1924), who defined it as a disturbance "in formative activities such as assembling, building and drawing, in which the spatial form of the product proves to be unsuccessful, without there being an apraxia of single movements." Visuoconstructive disabilities already had been described by earlier writers under the more general headings of "optic apraxia" and "optic ataxia," terms used to designate virtually any disturbance in performance referable to defective visual guidance of action. Thus awkwardness in the execution of acts requiring manual dexterity, inability to maintain one's balance in tests of locomotion, and defective imitation of movements, as well as visuoconstructive disabilities were considered to be forms of optic apraxia. Kleist singled out constructional apraxia as a separate disorder because of his conviction that it possessed a distinctive neuropsychological significance.

As Kleist's definition indicates, "constructional praxis" is a broad concept which has been applied to a number of rather different types of activities. These activities have in common the characteristic that they require the patient to assemble, join, or draw parts to form a single, unitary structure. However, they differ from each other in many respects, e.g., in complexity, in the type of movement and the degree of motor dexterity required in achieving the task, in the demands made on the higher intellectual functions, and in whether they involve construction in two or three spatial dimensions.

The most elementary constructional praxis tasks involve the utilization of elementary units to form rather simple two-dimensional structures, such as making a design out of sticks or building a simple vertical structure (e.g., tower, cross, pyramid) out of blocks. However, the difficulty of this type of task can be augmented to any desired level by requiring the subject to construct more complex patterns with mosaics or blocks, as in the block design tests of Kohs and Wechsler. Constructional deficits which are not apparent in a patient's performance on the simpler tasks are often reflected in failure on the more complex ones.

Because of their convenience, drawing tasks are often employed as tests of constructional praxis: the patient is required to copy figures, designs, or representations of varying degrees of complexity. The presented task may be a very easy one from the normative standpoint, as in the copying of simple geometric figures; or it may be on a somewhat higher level of difficulty, as in copying the three-figure designs of the Visual Retention Test (Benton, 1974) or the "complex figure" of Rey (1941). Again, visuoconstructional deficits not evident in performance on simpler drawing tasks may be brought to light by performance on these more complex tasks. However, it should be borne in mind that the task of copying designs includes a specific graphomotor component which is not found in other tasks designed to assess "constructional praxis."

Whatever their differences with respect to level of difficulty and type of activity required, all these tasks are essentially similar in that they involve the formation of two-dimensional structures, i.e., they assess two-dimensional constructional praxis. However, in his classic book on the parietal lobes, Critchley (1953, pp: 187–188) commented that:

> It is possible, and indeed useful, to proceed to problems in three-dimensional space though tests of this character are only too rarely employed. This is a more difficult undertaking, and patients who respond moderately well to the usual procedures with sticks and pencil-and-paper may display gross abnormalities when told to assemble bricks according to a three-dimensional pattern . . . The clinical story as given by the patient himself rarely affords any hint as to the existence of this three-dimensional constructional apraxia.

Critchley then described some unstandardized block-construction tasks which he employed for this purpose and presented illustrations of the performances of patients with three-dimensional constructional apraxia on these tasks.

The suggestion of Critchley that the evaluation of three-dimensional constructional praxis in the clinical neuropsychological examination may have distinctive diagnostic significance provided the impetus for us to develop a standardized procedure to assess the capacity (cf. Benton and Fogel, 1962). Later, a revised version incorporating certain changes in procedure which improved the test from both the psychometric and clinical standpoints was developed (cf. Benton, 1968a). In recent years we have developed a second form of the test which is equivalent in level of difficulty to the first form and we have collected normative and clinical data on a special administration of the test in which photographs of the block models, instead of the actual block models, are used as stimuli. These advances are incorporated in the version of the test described below.

When Kleist described constructional apraxia, he advanced the idea that the crucial lesion was in the posterior area of the left hemisphere. At first this localization was accepted and the close association of constructional apraxia with other deficits referable to left hemisphere disease, such as finger agnosia, right–left disorientation, and aphasic disturbances, was repeatedly noted. However, as early as the 1930s, the observation had been made that visuconstructive disability also could be shown by patients with lesions apparently confined to the right hemisphere. Thus it became evident that the deficit could not be exclusively related to left hemisphere disease. Subsequent studies demonstrated an impressively high incidence of visuoconstructive disabilities in patients with right hemisphere lesions and this led to a shift of opinion regarding the relative importance of the two hemispheres in mediating visuoconstructive performances (cf. McFie, Piercy & Zangwill, 1950; Hécaen, Ajuriaguerra & Massonet, 1951; Hécaen, Penfield, Bertrand & Malmo, 1956). In contrast to the earlier view, which regarded the deficit as a sign of disease of the dominant hemisphere, emphasis was placed on the crucial role of lesions of the right hemisphere in producing the picture of constructional apraxia. From an empirical standpoint, it now seems evident that there is a trend for patients with right hemisphere lesions to show a higher frequency of deficit, and more severe deficit, than do those with disease of the left hemisphere (cf. Benton, 1967; 1968b, 1979).

However, it has not been easy to identify the basis for this trend which, in any case, is reflected in relatively modest differences in the frequency of visuoconstructional defect shown by patients with lesions of the right and left hemispheres. A straightforward concept of "dominance" of the right hemisphere for visuoconstructive functions, analogous to the "dominance" of the left hemisphere for language functions in righthanded persons, is untenable; too many patients with left hemisphere disease show constructional apraxia. One proffered explanation is that there are two discrete types of visuoconstructive disability. One results from visuoperceptive impairment and is associated with disease of the right hemisphere; the other, which corresponds to the "true" constructional apraxia of Kleist, is an executive or perceptuomotor disability associated with disease of the left hemisphere. A good deal of investigative work has been devoted to the validation of this hypothesis but the question remains unresolved.

DESCRIPTION

Each form of the test (Form A and Form B) consists of three block models which are presented one at a time to the patient who is required to construct an exact replica of it by selecting the appropriate blocks from a set of loose blocks on a tray. The three models in each form are as follows:

Form A
Model I.   A pyramid made from six one-inch cubes (Fig. 11-1A)
Model II. An eight-block, four-level construction (Fig. 11-1B)
Model III. A fifteen-block, four-level construction (Fig. 11-2)
Form B
Model I.   A pyramidal structure of six blocks (Fig. 11-3A)
Model II. An eight-block, four-level construction (Fig. 11-3B)
Model III. A fifteen-block, four-level construction (Fig. 11-4)

Equivalence of Forms A and B   In the course of the clinical application of the test, it became apparent that at least one alternate form of equivalent difficulty

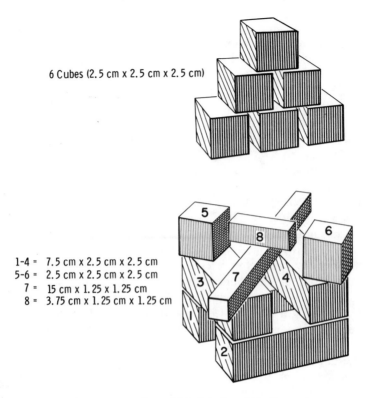

6 Cubes (2.5 cm x 2.5 cm x 2.5 cm)

1-4 = 7.5 cm x 2.5 cm x 2.5 cm
5-6 = 2.5 cm x 2.5 cm x 2.5 cm
7 = 15 cm x 1.25 x 1.25 cm
8 = 3.75 cm x 1.25 cm x 1.25 cm

Fig. 11-1 Schematic representation of Models I and II, Form A.

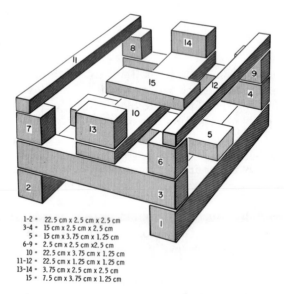

1-2 = 22.5 cm x 2.5 cm x 2.5 cm
3-4 = 15 cm x 2.5 cm x 2.5 cm
5 = 15 cm x 3.75 cm x 1.25 cm
6-9 = 2.5 cm x 2.5 cm x2.5 cm
10 = 22.5 cm x 3.75 cm x 1.25 cm
11-12 = 22.5 cm x 1.25 cm x 1.25 cm
13-14 = 3.75 cm x 2.5 cm x 2.5 cm
15 = 7.5 cm x 3.75 cm x 1.25 cm

Fig. 11-2 Schematic representation of Model III, Form A.

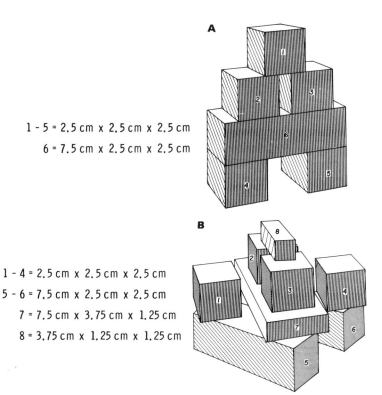

A

1 - 5 = 2.5 cm x 2.5 cm x 2.5 cm

6 = 7.5 cm x 2.5 cm x 2.5 cm

B

1 - 4 = 2.5 cm x 2.5 cm x 2.5 cm

5 - 6 = 7.5 cm x 2.5 cm x 2.5 cm

7 = 7.5 cm x 3.75 cm x 1.25 cm

8 = 3.75 cm x 1.25 cm x 1.25 cm

Fig. 11-3   Schematic representation of Models I and II, Form B.

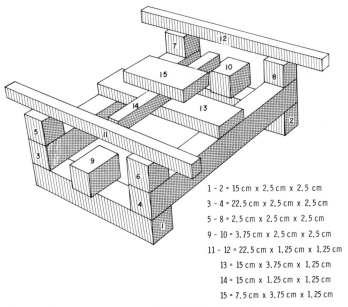

1 - 2 = 15 cm x 2.5 cm x 2.5 cm

3 - 4 = 22.5 cm x 2.5 cm x 2.5 cm

5 - 8 = 2.5 cm x 2.5 cm x 2.5 cm

9 - 10 = 3.75 cm x 2.5 cm x 2.5 cm

11 - 12 = 22.5 cm x 1.25 cm x 1.25 cm

13 = 15 cm x 3.75 cm x 1.25 cm

14 = 15 cm x 1.25 cm x 1.25 cm

15 = 7.5 cm x 3.75 cm x 1.25 cm

Fig. 11-4   Schematic representation of Model III, Form B.

TABLE 11-1   Three-Dimensional Block Construction: Mean Scores
(30 patients in each group)

	Block model presentation		Photographic presentation	
	Form A	Form B	Form A	Form B
Mean	25.4	24.5	20.7	20.2
Standard deviation	7.4	8.5	8.8	8.0
Mean difference	.9*		.5*	

*Nonsignificant

level was required in order to compare a patient's performance on successive occasions or to assess his performance when photographs (instead of the block models) are utilized as stimuli. It was for this reason that Form B was developed and its comparability to Form A was investigated.

The standardization sample consisted of four groups of 30 patients each. In each group, 10 patients were without history or evidence of cerebral disease, 10 patients had disease of the left hemisphere, and 10 patients had disease of the right hemisphere. The mean ages of the groups ranged from 43 to 48 years and were not significantly different from each other. Group I received Form A with the block model presentation; Group II received Form B with the block model presentation; Group III received Form A with the photographic presentation; Group IV received Form B with the photographic presentation.

The mean scores, standard deviations, and differences between mean scores are presented in Table 11-1. It will be seen that the difference between the mean scores of Groups I and II for the block model presentation of Forms A and B is very small and nonsignificant. Similarly, the difference in mean scores of Groups III and IV for the photographic presentation of Forms A and B is also very small and nonsignificant. These findings provide substantial evidence that Forms A and B are equivalent in respect to level of difficulty.

ADMINISTRATION

The entire set of 29 loose blocks is placed on a tray to the right or left of the subject, generally depending on his own preference. If lateral visual field defects are present, the blocks should be presented on the side of the unaffected field. The blocks are displayed in the standard arrangement shown in Figure 11-5. This arrangement should be restored before a new model is presented. Only the model to be copied is exposed; the other models remain hidden from the subject's view. The model is set before the subject and the following instructions are given:

Fig. 11-5 Arrangement of blocks placed before subject.

"Use these blocks and put some of them together so that they look like this model. Make the model as it looks as you face it, as you see it, not as I see it. You will not need all the blocks here and you will have to pick out the ones you need to make a copy of the model. Make your model as carefully as you can. This is more important than how long you take. Place the blocks in the same position and with the same angles as they are in the model. Tell me when you are finished."

The subject is permitted to pick up the blocks and inspect them. His understanding of the instructions should be checked during his construction, if this seems indicated. On rare occasion, a patient will try to match the model also with respect to the grain or color of the wooden blocks; he should be told to disregard differences in grain and color. Time taken for the construction of each model is recorded in seconds. Maximum time allowed for each model is 5 minutes. If the subject does not finish his construction within this time, the model is removed, the arrangement of loose blocks is restored, and the next model is presented.

The examiner should elicit from the subject an indication as to when he is finished with the construction of each model. The model is scored after the subject indicates that he is finished. Corrections made after this time are disregarded in the scoring.

The instructions in the original version of the test required the subject to use only one hand in building the constructions. This was done in order to make the motor skill component of the task equivalent for patients with or without hemiplegia. However, the procedure sometimes did not work well in practice, particularly in bedside testing. Many patients, having placed a block with one hand, feel the need to use the other hand to assist in the fine motor adjustments required for accurate positioning. Moreover, restriction to the use of one hand did not equate the motor skill component for hemiplegic patients who were forced to use their nonpreferred hand as compared to those who could use the preferred hand. For these reasons, the instructions were liberalized to permit the use of either or both hands in constructing the models. If a hemiplegic patient shows obvious difficulty in final positioning of a block, our practice has been to assist him so that he can proceed with the construction. In some circumstances, e.g., when the question of callosal disconnection has been raised, the examiner may wish to compare performances with the right and left hands. The use of Form A with one hand and Form B with the other hand should help reduce practice effects in this procedure.

Photographic Models   Photographic reproductions of the three block models are used as stimulus cards in this experimental version of the test. The photographs show the block models at about the same viewing angle as in Figures 11-1 to 11-4. The same administration is followed as for the block model administration. The photographs are shown to the subject one at a time and should be held upright or placed against a book or other support.

SCORING

One point is credited for each block that is placed correctly. Thus, perfect scores on the test models are 6, 8, and 15 points, respectively. The types of errors made in the construction of each model are recorded in addition to the overall "number correct" score. The following types of errors may occur: (1) omissions; (2) additions; (3) substitutions; (4) displacements (angular deviations, separations, misplacements).

For each model, the number and type of errors are recorded on the record sheet:

1. *Omissions.* Omission of one or more blocks from the constructed design.
2. *Additions.* Placement of one or more blocks beyond the number required.

Sometimes a subject will produce an unconnected arrangement of loose blocks. In this case, the examiner should ask the subject to indicate which blocks were intended to constitute the attempted construction.

3. *Substitutions*. Substitution of a block of incorrect size or shape in place of one of the blocks in the model. Each substitution is counted as one error, including the interchange of two or more blocks.

4. *Displacements*. The following criteria are used to evaluate displacement errors:
   A. Angular deviations (rotations) of 45° or greater, as estimated by visual inspection. Rotation of the whole construction or a minor rotation of an individual block are not counted as errors.
   B. Separations and misplacements are recorded when one or more blocks are placed in incorrect parts of the design, outside the design, if one or more blocks of the design are connected with the block model, or if no space is allowed between blocks which are spaced apart in the model. Minor displacements, e.g., poorly centered blocks, blocks which are farther apart than in the model, etc., are *not* counted as errors.

If the subject should construct the entire model with a rotated orientation, he should be reminded to make the model as *he* sees it. His construction should be scored in the usual manner as if it were not rotated, but the fact and degree of rotation should be noted.

In assessing performance, score the fewest number of errors as possible, i.e., the smallest number of errors which, if corrected, would produce a perfect construction. For example, incorrect angular placement of a block often involves a separation error as well. However, since correct placement of this single block would eliminate both errors, only one point is subtracted from total score and only one displacement error is noted.

Severely Defective Performance   A subject may place only a few blocks in an arrangement which only vaguely resembles the design. In this case, it is sometimes impossible to count individual types of errors. The score should be determined by counting the number of correctly placed blocks.

Time-Corrected Score   Count the total number of blocks placed correctly on Models I, II, and III. If the total time taken for constructing the three models exceeds 380 seconds, 2 points are subtracted from this sum. The corrected sum constitutes the score given to the performance.

Scoring Samples   Figure 11-6 shows a number of scoring samples for each of the three models to familiarize the examiner with some of the errors that can be made.

Model I (top left, compare with Fig. 11-1A): (1) substitution of a block of different shape; (2) displacement error; blocks on second layer are not separated. Total score: 6 − 2 = 4.

Model II (top right, compare with Fig. 11-1B): displacement, i.e., rotation of four blocks in bottom and second layer in relation to the blocks on top layer and in relation to the subject. Total score: 8 − 4 = 4.

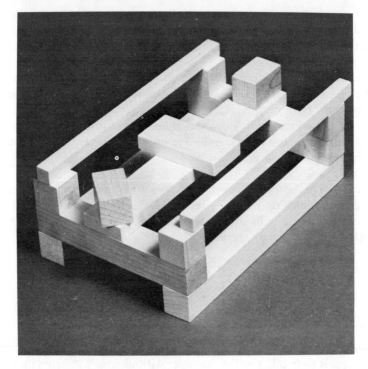

Fig. 11-6 Scoring samples (see text).

TABLE 11-2   Block Model Presentation: Distributions of Scores in Control and Brain-Diseased Patients

Score	Controls (n=100)	Brain-diseased total sample (n=40)	Right lesions (n=20)	Left lesions (n=20)
29	78	12	5	7
28	12	4	–	4
27	5	4	3	1
26	4	7	3	4
25	1	3	2	1
24	–	1	–	1
23	–	1	1	–
22	–	1	–	1
21	–	–	–	–
20	–	–	–	–
19	–	–	–	–
18	–	–	–	–
17	–	–	–	–
16	–	–	–	–
8–15	–	7	6	1

Model III (bottom, compare with Fig. 11-2): (1) omission of block on second layer; (2) displacements of blocks on top layer. Total score: $15 - 3 = 12$.

NORMATIVE OBSERVATIONS

Block Model Presentation   Table 11-2 shows the distribution of scores of a group of 100 control patients on the medical and surgical services of the University Hospital, Iowa City. They suffered from a variety of somatic disorders but showed no evidence or history of brain disease or injury. All patients were within the age range of 16–63 years. No patient with a history of seizures, head trauma followed by unconsciousness, or hospitalization for a psychiatric disorder or mental deficiency was included in this group. Mean age of the group was 42 years and mean educational level was 10 years.

It will be seen that 78 of the 100 patients made errorless performances and that an additional 12 patients made one error. Only 10 patients made 3–5 errors. Most of the errors made by the control patients consisted of an omission of one or more blocks in their construction, the most frequent omission being a failure to include the wide flat block in the lower part of the 15-block model, i.e., block no. 5 in Model III, Form A (Fig. 11-2) or block no. 13 in Model III, Form B (Fig. 11-4). Errors of substitution were rarely observed.

Photographic Presentation   Table 11-3 shows the distribution of scores of a group of 100 control patients without history or evidence of brain disease when

TABLE 11-3   Photographic Presentation: Distributions of Scores of Control and Brain-Diseased Patients

Score	Controls			Brain Diseased		
	Men (n=42)	Women (n=58)	Total (n=100)	Total sample (n=40)	Right lesions (n=20)	Left lesions (n=20)
29	16	27	43	3	1	2
28	7	5	12	–	–	–
27	10	14	24	4	2	2
26	3	4	7	1	1	–
25	3	3	6	2	1	1
24	2	–	2	3	1	2
23	–	1	1	1	–	1
22	–	1	1	3	1	2
21	1	–	1	2	–	2
20	–	1	1	2	1	1
19	–	1	1	3	–	3
18	–	–	–	2	1	1
17	–	1	1	1	–	1
16	–	–	–	1	1	–
15	–	–	–	1	1	–
14	–	–	–	2	2	–
13	–	–	–	1	1	–
12	–	–	–	1	–	1
11	–	–	–	–	–	–
10	–	–	–	–	–	–
5–9	–	–	–	7	6	1

they made constructions on the basis of photographs of the models. Forty-three patients made errorless performances and 12 patients made one error. Obviously the task is more difficult than the task of constructing from a block model, as reflected in a lower frequency of perfect or near-perfect performances, a lower mean score (27.3 for photographs, 28.6 for block models), and a wider range of scores (17–29 for photographs, 25–29 for block models).

As Table 11-3 shows, there was no difference in the proportion of men and women making two or more errors. However, there is a suggestion that women may be more variable than men: a higher proportion of women made either perfect scores or very poor scores.

The influence of educational level on performance when the constructions are made on the basis of photographs was assessed in a study by Benton and Ellis (1970). A sample of 80 control patients was divided into those with 11 or more years of schooling (n=52) and those with 10 or fewer years of schooling (n=28) and the performances of the two groups were compared. Differences in favor of the better-educated group were found. The mean score of the "high education"

TABLE 11-4   Three-Dimensional Block Construction: Scores of Children*

Age	n	Mean	Median	Range	5th percentile	10th percentile
6 years	12	21.8	21.1	14–28	–	18
7 years	50	23.3	23.6	15–29	15	19
8 years	43	24.2	24.5	18–29	18	20
9 years	38	25.5	26.0	18–29	19	21
10 years	40	26.1	26.2	19–29	22	23
11 years	39	26.0	26.2	19–29	21	23
12 years	37	26.8	27.2	23–29	23	24

*Adapted from Spreen & Gaddes (1969)

group was 28.0, while that of the "low education" group was 26.2. In the "high education" group, 73% made 0–1 error but only 32% of the "low education" group attained this level of performance.

The findings of this study also indicated that age was related to performance level, because older patients made a slightly higher number of errors than younger patients. The mean score of the patients below the age of 50 years ($n=61$) was 27.6 while the mean score of the patients who were 50 years or older ($n=19$) was 26.6. That this difference is not wholly attributable to the generally lower education level of the older patients was shown by a comparison of the two age groups when educational level was controlled. The proportion of patients under the age of 50 with 11 or more years of schooling who made 0–1 error was 78%; the corresponding proportion of patients who were 50 years or older with 11 years of schooling was 43%. Of the patients with 10 years of schooling or less, 0–1 error was made by 38% of the younger patients and 25% of the older patients.

Performances of Children   Normative data have been derived from the study of Spreen and Gaddes (1969) in which the test was given to 259 children in the age range of 6–12 years. The sample represented a random selection of children in a number of schools in Victoria, British Columbia, the only criteria for exclusion being that children who had repeated a grade and those with known learning problems, conduct disorders, or "brain dysfunction" were not tested. The mean IQ of about 112 for the sample approximated the mean IQ of 109 for the children of the Victoria school district.

Table 11-4 shows the mean and median scores for each age and the 5th and 10th percentile scores for ages 7–12. There is a progressive increase in mean score with advancing age, but also great variability within each age group. At the one extreme, two 7-year-old children made perfect scores; at the other extreme, two 12-year-olds made scores of 23. The mean and median scores of the 12-year-old sample are two points below the comparable statistics for adult subjects. It seems probable that the adult level of performance would be reached at about age 14.

PERFORMANCES OF PATIENTS WITH BRAIN DISEASE

Block Model presentation   In an early study in which performance on only the second and third block models was scored, Benton and Fogel (1962) found that 26 of 100 patients with brain disease (age range: 16–60 years) performed at a level lower than that of 99% of controls. Eight (40%) of the 20 patients with bilateral disease, 6 (14%) of the 43 patients with left hemisphere disease, and 12 (32%) of the 37 patients with right hemisphere disease performed defectively. The left hemisphere sample included four moderately aphasic patients. Thus this initial study indicated that defective three-dimensional constructional praxis was not a rare occurrence in patients with brain disease, and its frequency was likely to be particularly high in patients with bilateral or right hemisphere disease.

In a second study, the test was given to 40 patients (age range: 19–64 years) with diagnoses of disease confined to one or the other hemisphere (Keller, 1971). Twenty patients had lesions of the left hemisphere and 20 had lesions of the right hemisphere. The distribution of scores in this group of unilaterally brain-damaged patients is shown in Table 11-2. It will be seen that 12 patients (30%) made perfect constructions and 4 made only one error. The frequency of defective performance was relatively high. Thirteen patients (32.5%) made scores of 25 or less (i.e., scores exceeded by 99% of control patients). Again, it is evident that impairment in three-dimensional constructional praxis is not a rare finding in patients with brain disease.

It is also evident that the defective performances of the patients with brain disease fall into two distinct categories. Six patients (15%) made scores of 22–25, which may be considered to be moderately defective. On the other hand, the remaining seven patients who showed impairment (18%) made grossly defective performances (scores of 8–15); in most cases, their constructions were not recognizable replicas of the presented models.

Comparison of the performances of the patients with right and left hemisphere lesions again shows that failure was more frequent and more severe in the right hemisphere group. The overall frequency of failure was 45% in the right hemisphere group and 20% in the left hemisphere group. The between-group difference was particularly striking with respect to severely defective performances (scores of 8–15): the frequency of failure was 30% in the right hemisphere group and 5% in the left hemisphere group.

A third study (Benton, 1973) evaluated the influence of aphasic disorder on the association between performance on the three-dimensional constructional praxis test and side of lesion in patients with unilateral cerebral disease. The performances of different groups of patients, defined in terms of side of lesion and presence or absence of expressive and receptive aphasic disorder, were compared. The major findings of the study are summarized in Table 11-5. Patients with disease of the right hemisphere (all of whom were nonaphasic) showed a relatively high frequency of constructional disability while, among the patients with disease of the left hemisphere, only those aphasics with receptive language defects showed

TABLE 11-5 Three-Dimensional Block Construction: Frequency of Defect in Aphasic and Nonaphasic Patients[1]

Classification	n	Frequency of Failure[2]		
Left hemisphere disease				
A. Aphasic with severe receptive defect	9	66.7%		
			50%	
B. Aphasic with moderate receptive defect	9	33.3		32.4%
C. Expressive aphasia only	8	12.5		
			12.5	
D. Not aphasic	8	12.5		
Right hemisphere disease				
E. Not aphasic	14	35.7		

[1]Adapted from Benton (1973).
[2]Performance level exceeded by 99% of control patients.

a high frequency of constructional disability. Aphasic patients with only expressive language defects showed a low frequency of constructional disability, as did nonaphasic patients with disease of the left hemisphere. Thus the results supported the concept that there are two discrete types of visuoconstructive disability which are associated with side of lesion, one being language related and the other not.

Photographic Presentation   The same group of 40 patients who had been given the block model presentation were also given the photographic presentation with an alternate form of the test, i.e., those who received Form A with the block model presentation were given Form B with the photographic presentation and vice versa. The two administrations of the test were separated by an interval of 10 minutes during which the patient performed another task.

   Table 11-3 shows the distribution of scores. As will be seen, grossly defective performances (i.e., below the level of the poorest control patient) were made by 13 patients with brain disease, i.e., 32.5% of the group. Sixteen patients (40%) made scores (18 or less) which can be considered defective from a normative standpoint (i.e., scores exceeded by 99% of control patients). Conversely, only 7.5% of the group made perfect performances, as compared to 43% of the control patients. In general, the photographic presentation of the test poses a difficult task to the patient with brain disease.

Distinctive Performance Characteristics   Unusual constructions are sometimes made by patients with brain disease. The patient may appear at a loss as to how to proceed and finally succeed only in integrating a few components into a very

TABLE 11-6   Three-Dimensional Block Construction: Record Form

Name _____ No. _____ Date _____

Age _____ Sex _____ Education _____ Handedness _____ Examiner _____

			Presentation			
Form			**BLOCKS**	**PHOTOGRAPH**		
A	B					TOTAL
Total Time (sec) =				Model		
			I	II	III	
1. Omissions						
2. Additions						
3. Substitutions						
4. Gross Rotations						
5. Gross Displacements						
Number of Correctly Placed Blocks						

(If Total Time > 380 seconds, subtract 2 points from Total Score)

Total Score with Time Correction

NOTES

simple structure (Fig. 11-7A). A remarkable type of error is the so-called "closing-in" phenomenon in which the patient utilizes a part of the model to be copied in making his construction (Fig. 11-7B). Another remarkable type of error is partial or complete failure to build one half of the construction; at the same time the patient appears to believe that he has made a complete construction (Fig. 11-8). This type of performance is quite evidently an expression of unilateral spatial inattention or neglect (cf. Heilman, 1979).

For the most part, these unusual constructions are made by patients with lesions of the right hemisphere. Whether they represent defects in "perception" or in "execution" remains a question which has not been completely resolved. It is

Fig. 11-7 Illustrative constructions: (A) simplified structure; (B) "closing-in" phenomenon.

probable that they reflect a basic impairment in visuospatial orientation. A three-dimensional constructional praxis task may bring out this impairment in a patient who has no complaints in this regard and who performs adequately on other tasks.

CONCLUDING COMMENTS

A question that may be raised concerns the extent to which failure on this construction test is related to general mental impairment. The test presumably calls on the specific ability to assemble components in correct spatial relations to each other, but it also demands sustained attention and capacity for planned activity, which are abilities that are likely to be impaired in any patient suffering from general mental inefficiency as a consequence of brain disease.

The question is of some clinical importance since, if failure on the test is only an expression of general mental impairment, it is difficult to see how it can have a specific localizing significance, despite the empirical indications of a relatively close relationship between the deficit and lesions of the right hemisphere in nonaphasic patients. At the same time, given the presence of a significant general factor which pervades all mental performances, it may be expected that level of performance on the test will show some degree of relationship to general intellectual level. One would be surprised if demented patients were not inferior to more intact patients on this test (or, indeed, on any other performance). The crucial question is whether the demented patient is necessarily apraxic and, conversely, whether the apraxic patient is necessarily demented.

We have tried to answer this question for three-dimensional constructional praxis by classifying our patients with brain disease as "impaired" or "unimpaired" and determining the frequency of failure on the test in each group. We adopted as a criterion of general mental impairment a WAIS Verbal Scale IQ score which was 20 or more points below the IQ score to be expected on the basis of the age and education of the patient. An earlier normative study had shown that, in a group of 100 control patients, one could expect that two would show a discrepancy of 20 points between the observed IQ and the expected IQ (Fogel, 1964). In a group of 100 patients with brain disease, 35 showed discrepancy scores ranging from 20 to 49 points. These formed the impaired group and the remaining 65 patients (with discrepancy scores of 19 or less) formed the unimpaired group.

Thirty-seven of these 100 patients showed at least moderate defect on the test of three-dimensional constructional praxis (block model presentation), that is, their performance level was exceeded by 95% of a group of control patients. It was found that 21 (60%) of the 35 patients with general mental impairment performed defectively on the block constructions as compared to 16 (25%) of the 65 unimpaired patients. Clearly there was a positive association between three-dimensional constructional apraxia and the presence of general mental impairment in these patients with brain disease. However, 40% of the impaired patients performed adequately on the test; therefore it may be concluded that general mental impairment does not necessarily lead to visuoconstructive deficits

Fig. 11-8 Illustrative constructions: partial or complete failure to build left side of model.

of this type. Indeed, since 25% of the unimpaired patients performed defectively on the test, it is evident that the constructional disability may appear in the absence of general mental impairment.

Thus our results confirmed the observations of Arrigoni and De Renzi (1964) that constructional apraxia is significantly associated with general mental impairment. However, our findings that three-dimensional constructional apraxia may be observed in patients who do not suffer from general mental impairment indicate that a generalized intellectual deficit is not a necessary precondition for the appearance of this type of constructional apraxia. Finally, our observations indicated that many patients with fairly severe general mental impairment do not show these visuoconstructive difficulties.

The photographic presentation was developed with the thought that it might elicit failing performance in some brain-diseased patients who succeeded on the block model task. More specifically, it was felt that the photographic presentations might be particularly effective in identifying patients with right hemisphere lesions who so often experience difficulty in depth perception and stereopsis (cf. Benton and Hécaen, 1970; Carmon and Bechtoldt, 1969; Hamsher, 1978). The meager findings to date provide little support for these ideas. The photographic presentation did elicit a larger number of failing performances in the patients with right hemisphere lesions than in those with left hemisphere lesions (12 out of 20 vs. 9 out of 20). But the three instances in which the patients succeeded with block models and failed with the photographic presentations were not impressive, for in fact each of these patients performed on a borderline level with the block models. The only case exhibiting a striking dissociation was a patient with left hemisphere disease who performed perfectly on the block models but made a score of only 12 on the photographic presentation.

However, the photographic presentation may prove to be useful for some clinical and investigative purposes, e.g., in the assessment of a patient with vague complaints suggestive of brain dysfunction who performs within normal limits on a standard test battery, or in probing for the presence of impaired stereoscopic perception. In any case, the capacity of the photographic presentation to identify patients with focal brain disease is as high as (and possibly somewhat higher than) the block model presentation.

REFERENCES

Arrigoni G. & De Renzi E. (1964) Constructional apraxia and hemispheric locus of lesion. *Cortex 1*: 170–197.

Benton A. L. (1967) Constructional apraxia and the minor hemisphere. *Conf. Neurol. 29*: 1–16.

Benton A. L. (1968a) *Test de Praxie Constructive Tri-Dimensionnelle*, Paris. Editions du Centre de Psychologie Appliquée.

Benton A. L. (1968b) Differential behavioral effects in frontal lobe disease. *Neuropsychologia 6*: 53–60.

Benton A. L. (1973) Visuoconstruction disability in patients with cerebral disease: its relationship to side of lesion and aphasic disorder. *Doc. Ophthal. 33*: 67–76.

Benton A. L. (1974) *The Visual Retention Test*, (4th Ed). New York: The Psychological Corporation.

Benton A. L. (1979) Visuoperceptive, visuospatial, and visuoconstructive disorders. In *Clinical Neuropsychology*, K. M. Heilman & E. Valenstein (eds). New York: Oxford University Press, pp. 186–232.

Benton A. L. & Ellis E. (1970) Test de praxie tri-dimensionnelle: observations normatives concernant la performance au test lorsque les stimuli sont des photographies de construction modèles. *Rev. Psychol. Appl. 20*: 255–258.

Benton A. L. & Fogel M. L. (1962) Three-dimensional constructional praxis: a clinical test. *Arch. Neurol. 7*: 347–354.

Benton A. L. Hécaen H. (1970) Stereoscopic vision in patients with unilateral cerebral disease. *Neurology 20*: 1084–1088.

Carmon A. & Bechtoldt H. P. (1969) Dominance of the right hemisphere for stereopsis. *Neuropsychologia 7*: 29–39.

Critchley M. (1953) *The Parietal Lobes*. London: Edward Arnold.

Fogel M. L. (1964) The intelligence quotient as an index of brain damage. *Am. J. Orthopsychiat. 34*: 555–562.

Hamsher K. de S. (1978) Stereopsis and unilateral brain disease. *Inv. Ophthal. Vis. Sci. 17*: 336–343.

Hécaen H., Ajuriaguerra J. & Massonet J. (1951) Les troubles visuoconstructive par lésion pariéto-occipitale droite. *Encéphale 40*: 122–179.

Hécaen H., Penfield W., Bertrand C. & Malmo R. (1956) The syndrome of apractognosia due to lesions of the minor cerebral hemisphere. *Arch. Neurol. Psychiat. 75*: 400–434.

Heilman K. M. (1979) Neglect and related disorders. In *Clinical Neuropsychology*, K. M. Heilman & E. Valenstein (eds). New York: Oxford University Press, pp. 268–307.

Keller W. K. (1971) A comparison of two procedures for assessing constructional praxis in patients with unilateral cerebral disease. Ph.D. Dissertation, University of Iowa.

Kleist K. (1923) Kriegsverletzungen des Gehirns in ihrer Bedeutung für die Hirnlokalisation und Hirnpathologie. In *Handbuch der aerztlichen Erfahrung im Weltkriege 1914/1918, Bd. IV, Geistes-und Nervenkrankheiten*, O. von Schjerning (ed). Leipzig: Barth.

Kleist K. (1934) *Gehirnpathologie*. Leipzig: Barth.

McFie J., Piercy M. & Zangwill O. (1950) Visual spatial agnosia associated with lesions of the right hemisphere. *Brain 73*: 167–190.

Piercy M. F. & Smyth V. (1962) Right hemisphere dominance for certain nonverbal intellectual skills. *Brain 85*: 775–790.

Rey A. (1941) L'examen psychologique dans les cas d'encéphalopathie traumatique. *Arch. Psychol. 28*: 215–268.

Spreen O. & Gaddes W. H. (1969) Developmental norms for 15 neuropsychological tests age 6 to 15. *Cortex 5*: 170–191.

Strauss H. (1924) Ueber konstruktive Apraxie. *Mschr. Psychiat. 56*: 65–124.

Warrington E. K. (1969) Constructional apraxia. In *Handbook of Clinical Neurology*, Vol. 4, P. J. Vinken & G. W. Bruyn (eds). Amsterdam: North-Holland.

12. Motor Impersistence

Motor impersistence denotes the inability of some patients to sustain a movement which they were able to initiate on command, e.g., inability to *keep* the eyes closed or the tongue protruded, to *maintain* conjugate gaze steadily in a fixed direction, or to make a *prolonged* "ah" sound. Following earlier case reports describing the phenomenon (Oppenheim, 1895; Roth, 1901; Lewandowsky, 1907; Schilder, 1924; Pineas, 1924; Zutt, 1950), two fairly extensive studies appeared in the 1950s.

Berlin (1955) reported that he had seen 16 patients with right hemisphere disease who exhibited motor impersistence in the form of inability to keep the eyes closed, the tongue protruded, or the mouth open, on verbal command. Some showed evidence of general mental impairment, but others did not; therefore Berlin did not believe that mental impairment was a necessary part of the clinical picture. He found no evidence of the disability in 25 patients with left hemisphere disease.

Fisher (1956), who coined the term "motor impersistence" to designate the phenomenon, described 10 patients with left hemiplegia who showed diverse forms of impersistence. In addition to failure to sustain eyelid closure and tongue protrusion, some of these patients could not maintain central or lateral gaze fixation, hold their breath, make a prolonged "ah" sound, or exert steady hand-grip pressure. These patients were likely to show "more severe mental impairment" than patients with left hemiplegia who were not impersistent. Fisher further reported that "in most instances" motor impersistence was not found in patients with right hemiplegia.

These observations by Berlin and Fisher suggesting a specific association between motor impersistence and right hemisphere disease provided the impetus for Joynt, Benton, and Fogel (1962) to undertake a more systematic study, during the course of which they developed a standardized objective test to measure motor impersistence. Later, this test was utilized in studies by Benton, Garfield, and Chiorini (1964), Garfield (1964), Domrath (1966), Garfield, Benton, and MacQueen (1966), Ben-Yishay, Diller, Gerstman, and Haas (1968), Rutter, Graham, and Yule (1970), and Levin (1973a,b). The results of these studies, which analyze the performances of adults and children in diverse diagnostic categories, are discussed below.

DESCRIPTION AND ADMINISTRATION

The battery consists of eight tests requiring the maintenance of a movement or posture (Table 12-5). The administration and scoring of each test are as follows:

1. Keeping eyes closed   The patient is instructed to close his eyes and keep them closed. He is judged to have terminated his response if, at any time prior to the end of the trial, any part of the eyeball becomes visible. Fluttering of the lids is not counted as long as the lids remain closed. Two 20-second trials are given and the total score is the sum of seconds over which performance is sustained, a perfect score being 40. Verbatim instructions to the patient are as follows:

> *"This is the first thing we are going to do. I want you to close your eyes and keep them closed, until I tell you to open them. Ready, close your eyes."* (First trial of 20 seconds) *"Now, you can open them. We will do it again. When I tell you to, close your eyes and keep them closed. Ready, close your eyes."* (Second trial of 20 seconds) *"Now you can open them."*

2. Protruding tongue (blindfolded)   For this task, the patient is blindfolded and told to stick out his tongue and keep it out. He is judged to have terminated his response if, prior to the end of the trial, the tongue is retracted to a point posterior to the outer edge of the upper lip. Two 20-second trials are given, and total score determined in the same manner as on task 1. Verbatim instructions to the patient are as follows:

> *"Now this time I want you to stick your tongue out and keep it out, like this. I am going to put this mask over your face like this so that you cannot see.* (Examiner adjusts blindfold.) *There, is that OK? Remember, stick your tongue out and keep it out until I tell you to stop. Ready, stick your tongue out.* (First trial of 20 seconds) *Stop. Now we are going to do this one more time. Ready, stick out your tongue and keep it out.* (Second trial of 20 seconds) *Stop."*

3. Protruding tongue (eyes open)   The same procedure as for task 2 is followed except that the patient is not blindfolded. Verbatim instructions to the patient are as follows:

> *"Now we are going to do the same thing; this time I will take the mask off so that you can see.* (Examiner removes blindfold.) *Remember, stick out your tongue and keep it out. Ready, stick out your tongue.* (First trial of 20 seconds) *Stop. Now we are going to do this one more time. Ready, stick out your tongue and keep it out.* (Second trial of 20 seconds) *Stop."*

4. Fixation of gaze in lateral visual fields   With his head fixed in the midline position, the patient is instructed to look at the examiner's finger and to keep looking at it, as the examiner extends a finger vertically at approximately a 45 degree angle in the horizontal plane of the patient's right visual field for 30 seconds. The procedure is repeated in the patient's left visual field. Each time the patient looks away from the examiner's finger, one point is scored and the patient is reminded to keep looking at the finger. A point is not scored if, in the examiner's judgment, the patient makes eye movements directed at different points on the examiner's finger. Total score is the number of instances of looking away from the stimulus. A score of zero indicates perfect performance. Verbatim instructions to the patient are as follows:

> *"I want you to keep your head in this position.* (Examiner adjusts patient's head so that it is in the midline position) *I am going to hold up a finger, and I want you to look at it and keep looking right at it until I tell you to stop. Ready, go."* After 30 seconds, examiner says *"Now I am going to hold up a finger on the other side. Look at my finger and keep looking right at it until I tell you to stop. Ready, go."* (Second trial of 30 seconds.)

5. Keeping mouth open   The patient is instructed to open his mouth and keep it open. He is judged to have terminated his response, if prior to the end of the trial, the mouth returned to its pretrial position. Two 20-second trials are given, total score being determined in the same manner as on task 1. Verbatim instructions to the patient are as follows:

> *"Now when I tell you to, open your mouth and keep it open* (Examiner demonstrates) *until I tell you to stop. Ready, open your mouth.* (First trial of 20 seconds) *Stop. Now we are going to do this once more. Ready, open your mouth and keep it open.* (Second trial of 20 seconds) *Stop."*

6. Central fixation during confrontation testing of visual fields   The patient is instructed to look at the examiner's nose and to keep looking at it while the examiner gradually brings a finger around the side of the face, from a point in line with the patient's ears, until the finger has reached a point in a 45 degree angle in the horizontal plane of the patient's right or left visual field. Patient is told to tell examiner when he first sees the finger out of the corner of his eye. Each time the patient looks away from the examiner's nose, a point is scored. A point is not scored if, in the examiner's judgment, the patient engages in eye movements directed at different points on the examiner's nose. Each time the patient looks away from the examiner's nose, he is reminded to keep looking at it. Two trials of 20 seconds each are given for each visual field. Fields are tested in alternate order, beginning with the finger in the patient's right visual field. Total score is the number of points scored on all four trials. Verbatim instructions to the patient are as follows:

"When I tell you to begin, I want you to look right at my nose and <u>keep looking at it</u>. While you are doing that, I am going to bring my finger around the side of your face, like this (Examiner demonstrates) *and you tell me when you first see my finger out of the corner of your eye. But keep looking at my nose all the time until I tell you to stop. Ready, go."* After each vacillation, Examiner says, *"Keep looking at my nose."* After the first trial of 20 seconds in the right visual field, examiner says, *"Now, we are going to do the same thing with my finger on the other side. Keep looking at my nose, but tell me when you first see my finger out of the corner of your eye. Ready, go."* The same instruction is repeated through two further trials, one in the right visual field and the other in the left visual field.

7. Head turning during sensory testing   The patient is instructed to state which finger is being touched while the examiner touches each of the patient's fingers in random order. He is told to turn his head away and *not* look at his hand until told that the task is over. One point is scored if, in the examiner's judgment, the patient looks at his hand after the presentation of the stimulus and prior to the ensuing stimulus. A point is not scored if the patient turns his head but looks only at the examiner. After each scored response, the patient is reminded not to look at his hand. If, as occasionally happens, the patient asks the examiner what he should call each finger, he is told to call them whatever he thinks is appropriate, i.e., he is not instructed in the correct labeling of his fingers. No penalty is attached if the patient incorrectly names a finger. Two trials on each hand are given, with the hands tested alternately, beginning with the right. Total score is the number of points scored over the four trials. A perfect score is zero; poorest score is 20. Verbatim instructions to the patient are as follows:

"This time, will you put this (right) hand on the table. (Examiner demonstrates with fingers extended, palms down.) *I am going to touch each one of your fingers and you tell me each time which one I have touched. While we are doing this, I want you to look over there* (Examiner points to wall to patient's left), *and don't look at your hand until I tell you that we have finished. OK, here we go."* (If patient does not turn his head, examiner reminds him to do so.)

   After one trial with the right hand, the examiner says, *"Done. Now, we will do the same thing with your other hand. Turn your head away and do not look at your hand until I say we are finished. Here we go."* The same procedure is followed through a total of two trials with each hand.

8. Saying "ah"   After a demonstration, the patient is instructed to take a deep breath and say "ah," holding it as long as he can. The response is judged to have terminated when there is a cessation or interruption of phonation. The continuation of expiration following such a break is not scored, nor is the resumption of voiced speech once it was interrupted. Total score is the sum in seconds of the response on two trials. Verbatim instructions to the patient are as follows:

> *"Here is the last thing we are going to do. When we begin, I want you to take a deep breath and say 'ah.' Like this, I'll show you.* (Examiner takes breath, produces 'ah' for five seconds.) *But I want you to say 'ah,' as long as you can. OK, whenever you are ready, take a deep breath and say 'ah,' as long as you can."* After first trial, Examiner says, *"We will do this once more. Whenever you are ready, take a deep breath and say 'ah' as long as you can."*

NORMATIVE OBSERVATIONS

Adult Performance   The test battery was given to a group of 106 control patients from the medical and surgical services of the University Hospitals, Iowa City, who suffered from a variety of somatic disorders but who showed no evidence or history of brain disease. No patient with a history of seizures, head trauma followed by unconsciousness, or hospitalization for psychiatric disorder or mental deficiency was included in this group. All patients were within the age range of 16–66 years. Mean age of the group was 44.5 years and mean educational level was 10 years.

Eighty-nine (84%) of the 106 patients made error-free performances on all eight measures. Fifteen patients (14%) showed defective performances on one subtest. One patient showed defective performances on two subtests, and one patient showed defective performances on three subtests. These findings led to a categorization of defective results into two groups: failure on two or three subtests was considered to indicate "moderate impersistence" and failure on four or more subtests as "marked impersistence."

The following criteria for defective performance on each subtest were established:

> 1. *Keeping eyes closed.* Impersistence is defined as a total score of less than 36 which corresponds to a performance level below that of 98% of the control patients.
> 2. *Protruding tongue (blindfolded).* Impersistence is defined as any performance which was less than perfect, i.e., a performance level below that of 96% of the control patients.
> 3. *Protruding tongue (eyes open).* Impersistence is defined as any performance which was less than perfect, i.e., a performance level below that of all control patients.
> 4. *Fixation of gaze in lateral visual fields.* Impersistence is defined as the occurrence of two or more instances of failure to maintain fixation, i.e., a performance level below that of 98% of the control patients.
> 5. *Keeping mouth open.* Impersistence is defined as any performance which is less than perfect on either trial, i.e., a performance level below that of 99% of the control patients.
> 6. *Central fixation during confrontation testing of visual fields.* Impersistence is defined as a score of three or more points, i.e., a performance level below that of 96% of the control patients.

TABLE 12-1   Relative Frequency of Impersistence on Each Test in Children

Age, yrs. (n)		Test, % of impersistence*							
		1	2	3	4	5	6	7	8
5	(20)	10%	30%	15%	60%	25%	90%	70%	80%
6–7	(40)	2.5	17.5	7.5	25	12.5	70	47.5	57.5
8–9	(40)	0	15	10	17.5	5	55	22.5	30
10–11	(40)	2.5	2.5	2.5	10	2.5	25	5	25

*1. keeping eyes closed
2. protruding tongue (eyes closed)
3. protruding tongue (eyes open)
4. lateral fixation

5. keeping mouth open
6. central fixation
7. head turning
8. saying "ah"

7. *Head turning during sensory testing*. Impersistence is defined as less than perfect performance on all four trials, i.e., a performance level below that of 98% of the control patients.

8. *Saying "ah"*. Impersistence is defined as a score of less than 18 seconds, that is, a performance level below that of 94% of the control group.

Performances of children   Normative data have been derived from the study of Garfield (1963, 1964) in which the motor impersistence battery was given to 140 normal children seen in the Department of Pediatrics of University Hospitals, Iowa City. (The battery was modified in one respect. A time limit of 20 seconds, instead of 30 seconds, was imposed in Test 4—fixation of gaze in lateral visual fields.) The sample consisted of 10 boys and 10 girls at each of seven age levels, 5 through 11 years. No child was included in the sample who was acutely ill or under any restriction of activity for medical reasons, or who had a known history of neurological disease or injury. Mean WISC IQ of the sample was 102, range 80–119.

Table 12-1 shows the number of children in four age groups who showed impersistence on each subtest according to the adult criteria. As would be expected, there is a progressive rise in performance level with increasing age. The performances of children in the 10–11 years group are comparable to that of adults on six of the tests, the exceptions being Tests 6 and 8 (Central fixation during confrontation testing; Saying "ah").

Table 12-2 shows the proportion of children in each age group who failed two to three tests (moderate impersistence by adult standards) and four to six tests (marked impersistence by adult standards). As can be seen, "impersistence" is universal among five-year olds, is shown by about 50% of children in the 6–9 years age range, and is relatively infrequent among 10–11 year olds. Only one child in the 10–11 years group showed marked impersistence (failure on four or more tests).

TABLE 12-2   Percentages of Children Showing Motor Impersistence

Age, yrs.	(*n*)	Frequency of failure, %		
		2–3 tests	4–6 tests	2–6 tests
5	(20)	45	55	100
6–7	(40)	35	25	60
8–9	(40)	45	5	50
10–11	(40)	15	2.5	17.5

TABLE 12-3   Percentages of Children Failing Impersistence Subtests

Age, yrs. (*n*)		Number of tests failed						
		0	1	2	3	4	5	6
5	(20)	0%	0%	20%	25%	25%	20%	10%
6–7	(40)	10	30	17.5	17.5	15	10	0
8–9	(40)	22.5	27.5	27.5	17.5	5	0	0
10–11	(40)	52.5	30	12.5	2.5	2.5	0	0

TABLE 12-4   Performances of Children: Criteria of Motor Impersistence

Age, yrs.	Number of tests failed	
	Moderate impersistence	Marked impersistence
5	6	7+
6–7	5	6+
8–9	4	5+
10–11	3	4+

The number of tests failed by the children in each group is shown in greater detail in Table 12-3. Although by adult standards, all the 5-year-old children are impersistent, 90% of them performed normally on three or more tests. All of the children in the 6–7 years age group performed normally on three or more tests. Normal performances on four or more tests were made by all children in the 8–11 years range. Suggested criteria of defective performance in the several age groups are presented in Table 12-4.

PERFORMANCES OF PATIENTS WITH BRAIN DISEASE

In an early study of the behavioral and pathological correlates of motor impersistence, Joynt, Benton, and Fogel (1962) found that 23% of a sample of 101 patients with hemispheric brain disease were impersistent. Of these 23 patients, 11 showed moderate impersistence (failure on two to three tasks), and 12 showed marked impersistence (failure on four or more tasks). No striking differences in the frequency of defective performance were found when the sample was divided into subgroups comprised of patients with bilateral disease ($n=19$), right hemisphere disease ($n=34$), and left hemisphere disease ($n=48$). Impersistence was shown by 26% of the bilateral cases, 26% of the patients with right hemisphere lesions, and 19% of those with left hemisphere lesions. However, marked impersistence was shown by only 6% of the left hemisphere patients, as compared to 15% of the right hemisphere patients and 16% of the bilateral or diffuse patients.

A later study by Levin (1973a) of 32 patients with unilateral lesions found that 14 (44%) showed impersistence, with the proportions of cases showing moderate or marked impersistence being equal (22%). No hemispheric differences in the frequency of either moderate or marked impersistence were evident.

Both the Joynt and Levin studies found a somewhat higher frequency of motor impersistence in older patients. Joynt, Benton, and Fogel found that 26% of the patients who were 45 years or older were impersistent as compared to 21% of patients under the age of 45. Levin found that the mean age of his impersistent patients was 56 years as compared to a mean age of 47 years for the patients who performed normally.

PERFORMANCES OF BRAIN-DAMAGED CHILDREN

Garfield (1963, 1964) investigated motor impersistence in children with brain disease by comparing the performances of a group of 25 such children with 25 normal children, individually matched for age, sex, and WISC IQ. The mean age of the groups was 8 years, 6 months, and mean IQ was 94 (range 80–111). The criterion for inclusion of children in the brain-diseased group was a diagnosis of brain damage by a pediatric neurologist, substantiated by evidence of spastic or flaccid paralysis of the extremities due to a cerebral lesion. Children who had neuromuscular involvement of the body parts necessary for performance of the tests were excluded. The mean performance level of the brain-damaged group was lower than that of the controls on all eight tests, significantly so on six tests. The most discriminating tests were Numbers 4 (lateral fixation), 2 and 3 (protruding tongue), and 6 (central fixation). The least discriminating were Numbers 1 (keeping eyes closed) and 7 (head turning during sensory testing). Utilizing age-related normative standards of performance (instead of adult norms), Garfield found that 17 (68%) of the brain-damaged children were impersistent on two or more tests, as compared to 4 (3%) of the total group of 140 controls.

Rutter, Graham, and Yule (1970) found that five (71%) of seven children in the 9–10 year age range who had been judged to be neurologically impaired on the basis of clinical signs showed impersistence on the basis of age-related norms. In a sample of 108 retarded readers, 20 (19%) proved to be impersistent, as compared to 5% of control children.

PERFORMANCES OF MENTALLY RETARDED AND SCHIZOPHRENIC SUBJECTS

Benton, Garfield, and Chiorini (1964) investigated the performances of mentally retarded (mean IQ = 52) as compared to normal children of either equivalent chronological age or equivalent mental age. The retarded children were grossly inferior to normal children of the same age. When impersistence was defined as a performance level poorer than that of 95% of the normal children, the retarded children showed a high frequency of failure on every task that ranged from 38% (protruding tongue) to 90% (saying "ah"). Comparison of performances of retarded and normal children of the same *mental* age disclosed less striking differences. The retarded children were significantly inferior on only two tasks (keeping eyes closed, saying "ah"). However, a few of them showed a marked degree of motor impersistence that could not be accounted for by their relatively low mental age.

In their Isle of Wight study, Rutter, Graham, and Yule (1970) found a relatively high frequency of motor impersistence in a group of 9–10-year-old children with moderate or mild mental retardation (range of WISC IQs: 51–85). Specifically, 23% of the retarded children were more impersistent than 95% of normal children of the same age. Retarded children with evidence of brain damage were found by Garfield, Benton, and MacQueen (1966) to be more frequently impersistent than those of equivalent age and IQ who were in the cultural-familial category.

Domrath (1966) found that nine (15%) in a sample of 60 schizophrenic patients showed moderate impersistence (failure on 2–3 tasks) as compared to two (3%) in a sample of 60 control patients. None of the schizophrenic patients showed marked impersistence (failure on four or more tests).

CORRELATES

The early reports of Berlin and Fisher suggested that motor impersistence was specifically associated with right hemisphere disease. However, more systematic studies of the phenomenon failed to confirm this association. Joynt, Benton, and Fogel found only a slightly higher frequency of impersistence in patients with right hemisphere disease as compared to those with left lesions, although the between-hemisphere difference was somewhat higher for marked impersistence. Levin found no difference in the relative frequency of motor impersistence in right and left hemisphere damaged groups that were comparable in age, educational level, and type of lesion.

In contrast, a close relationship between motor impersistence and general mental impairment has been a consistent finding. This was Fisher's impression, but Berlin did not think that the association was important. Joynt, Benton, and Fogel divided their sample of 101 patients with brain disease into those ($n=31$) showing general mental impairment (as defined by an age-corrected WAIS IQ which was 20 or more points below expectations) and those ($n=70$) with IQs closer to expectations. Forty percent of the mentally impaired showed motor impersistence as compared to 16% of the unimpaired patients. In a study of 24 patients with left hemiplegia, Ben-Yishay, Diller, Gerstman, and Haas (1968), found rank-order correlation coefficients ranging from $-.43$ to $-.76$ between degree of motor impersistence and scores on seven WAIS subtests.

Joynt, Benton, and Fogel found a somewhat higher frequency of motor impersistence in patients who were 45 years of age or older as compared to younger patients. However, the difference between the two age groups was not significant. A small positive correlation between degree of motor impersistence and age was found by Ben-Yishay, Diller, Gerstman, and Haas (1968).

The predictive significance of motor impersistence for the outcome of rehabilitation in patients with left hemiplegia was investigated by Ben-Yishay and colleagues (1968), who found that those who were impersistent spent a longer time in the rehabilitation program and attained a lesser degree of functional competence as compared to patients who performed normally. Since the impersistent patients tended to be intellectually impaired, it is not clear that motor impersistence possesses a distinctive prognostic significance.

COMMENT

There are a number of unanswered questions associated with the phenomenon of motor impersistence. How to define the capacity measured by the tests is not settled, nor is it clear that all the tests measure the same capacity. Questions about reliability of the measures have also been raised.

There is a substantial degree of association between motor impersistence and the presence of general mental impairment in adult patients as well as between motor impersistence and low mental age in children and adolescents. Nevertheless, it is generally believed that motor impersistence reflects derangement of some specific mechanism. Many demented patients do not show the disability and some mentally retarded patients show a marked degree of impersistence that cannot be accounted for in terms of their low mental age.

Motor impersistence has been viewed as a form of apraxia, as resulting from impaired cortical control of movement, and as expression of a weakness in attention and concentration. Carmon (1970) postulated that motor impersistence occurred as a consequence of impaired utilization of proprioceptive information about the spatial location of one's body parts; and Levin (1973b) did find a relationship between the disability and performance on a proprioceptive feedback task in patients with right hemisphere disease but not in those with left hemisphere lesions.

TABLE 12-5   Motor Impersistence Record Form

Name _____ No. _____ Date _____

Age _____ Sex _____ Education _____ Handedness _____ Examiner _____

Keeping Eyes Closed
    trial 1 _____ seconds   trial 2 _____ seconds   Total _____ seconds   P   F
Protruding tongue (blindfolded)
    trial 1 _____ seconds   trial 2 _____ seconds   Total _____ seconds   P   F
Protruding tongue (eyes open)
    trial 1 _____ seconds   trial 2 _____ seconds   Total _____ seconds   P   F
Fixation of gaze in lateral visual fields
    trial 1 (R) _____ deviations   trial 2 (L) _____ deviations
    Total _____ deviations   P   F
Keeping mouth open
    trial 1 _____ seconds   trial 2 _____ seconds   Total _____ seconds   P   F
Central fixation during confrontation testing
    trial 1 (R) _____ points   trial 2 (L) _____ points
    trial 3 (R) _____ points   trial 4 (L) _____ points   Total _____ points   P   F
Head turning during sensory testing
    trial 1 (R) _____ points   trial 2 (L) _____ points
    trial 3 (R) _____ points   trial 4 (L) _____ points   Total _____ points   P   F
Saying "ah"
    trial 1 _____ seconds   trial 2 _____ seconds   Total _____ seconds   P   F

    TOTALS: _____ tests passed
               _____ tests failed
    Observations: _____

NORMAL   MODERATE   MARKED   (circle appropriate category)

Inter-judge agreement in scoring responses has been shown to be satisfactory (Garfield, 1964), but conflicting findings on retest reliability have been reported. Bell, Lewis, Diller, and Bell (1971) found that the rank order of scores was stable when the test was given on different occasions by different examiners, but Rutter, Graham, and Yule (1970) encountered several instances of discrepancies of two or more points in total score under a test–retest condition in which two different psychologists assessed the children. Moreover, Bell, Lewis, Diller, and Bell (1971) reported that, although total scores were reasonably stable from test to retest, there was less consistency in performance on the individual tests from test to retest. Their cluster analysis raised the question of whether there may be distinctive forms of motor impersistence.

REFERENCES

Bell D. B., Lewis F. D., Diller L. & Bell B. W. (1971) Puzzling impersistence of the motor impersistence test. *Proc. Am. Psychol. Assoc.* 6: 623–624.

Benton A. L., Garfield J. C. & Chiorini J. C. (1964) Motor impersistence in mental defectives. *Proceedings, International Congress on the Scientific Study of Mental Retardation (Copenhagen)*, pp. 746–750.

Ben-Yishay Y., Diller L., Gerstman L. & Haas A. (1968) The relationship between impersistence, intellectual function and outcome of rehabilitation in patients with left hemiplegia. *Neurology 18*: 852–861.

Ben-Yishay Y., Haas A. & Diller L. (1967) The effects of oxygen inhalation on motor impersistence in brain-damaged individuals: a double-blind study. *Neurology 17*: 1003–1010.

Berlin L. (1955) Compulsive eye opening and associated phenomena. *Arch. Neurol. Psychiat. 73*: 597–601.

Carmon A. (1970) Impaired utilization of kinesthetic feedback in right hemisphere lesions: possible implications for the pathophysiology of "motor impersistence". *Neurology 20*: 1033–1038.

Domrath R. P. (1966) Motor impersistence in schizophrenia. *Cortex 2*: 474–483.

Fisher M. (1956) Left hemiplegia and motor impersistence. *J. Nerv. Ment. Dis. 123*: 201–213.

Garfield J. C. (1963) Motor impersistence in normal and brain-damaged children. Unpublished Doctoral Dissertation, University of Iowa.

Garfield J. C. (1964) Motor impersistence in normal and brain-damaged children. *Neurology 14*: 623–630.

Garfield J. C., Benton A. L. & MacQueen J. C. (1966) Motor impersistence in brain-damaged and cultural-familial defectives. *J. Nerv. Ment. Dis. 142*: 434–440.

Joynt R. J., Benton A. L. & Fogel M. L. (1962) Behavioral and pathological correlates of motor impersistence. *Neurology 12*: 876–881.

Levin H. (1973a) Motor impersistence in patients with unilateral cerebral disease: a cross-validation study. *J. Consulting Clin. Psychol. 41*: 287–290.

Levin H. (1973b) Motor impersistence and proprioceptive feedback in patients with unilateral cerebral disease. *Neurology 23*: 833–841.

Lewandowsky M. (1907) Ueber Apraxie des Lidschlusses. *Berliner Medizinische Wochenschrift 44*: 921.

Oppenheim H. (1895) Zur Symptomatologie der Pseudobulbarparalyse. *Neurologisches Centralblatt 14*: 40–41.

Pineas H. (1924) Hirnbefunde bei Apraxie. *Zentralblatt fuer die gesamte Neurologie und Psychiatrie 35*: 446.

Roth W. C. (1901) Demonstration von Kranken mit Opthalmoplegie. *Neurologisches Centralblatt 20*: 921–923.

Rutter M., Graham P. & Yule W. (1970) *A Neuropsychiatric Study in Childhood*. London: Spastics International Medical Publications.

Schilder P. (1924) Die Encephalitis periaxialis diffusa (nebst Bemerkungen über die Apraxie des Lidschlusses). *Archiv fuer Psychiatrie 71*: 327–356.

Zutt J. (1950) Über die Unfähigheit die Augen geschlossen zu halten. Apraxie des Lidschlusses oder Zwangsblicken. *Nervenarzt 21*: 339–345.

Name Index

Subject Index

Age effects
  facial recognition, 33, 35, 38
  finger localization, 87, 90
  judgment of line orientation, 48–49
  motor impersistence, 133, 135
  right–left orientation, 13–14
  serial digit learning, 23–24, 26–27
  tactile form perception, adults, 74–76
  tactile form perception, children, 78–80
  temporal orientation, 5
  three-dimensional block construction, 117
  visual form discrimination, 58
Agnosia. *See also* Prosopagnosia
  for faces, 30–31
  visual, 30
Agnosia, facial. *See* Prosopagnosia
Alexia. *See* Aphasia
Amnesia
  digit span performance, 23
  serial digit learning, 13
  temporal orientation, 3
Aphasia
  assessment of, 60–61, 63
  auditory discrimination, 98
  confusion in, 100
  constructional apraxia and, 106
  deviant response set, 100
  facial recognition, 39–42
  finger localization, 93–95
  judgment of line orientation, 49–52
  pantomime recognition, 63–65, 67–68
  recovery of function in, 59, 63
  right–left orientation, 10, 15–16; systematic
    reversals in, 13
  tactile form perception, 78, 80–81
  temporal orientation, 7
  three-dimensional block construction perfor-
    mance, 118–19
  visual form discrimination, 59–60; recovery
    of, 59

Astereognosis. *See* Tactile form perception
Attention defects
  finger localization, 85
  serial digit learning, 25
  three-dimensional block construction, 122
  visual form discrimination, 59
Aural comprehension (and impairment of). *See
  also* Pantomime recognition; Reading
  comprehension; Token Test
  components of, 98
  facial recognition, 39–41
  Kleist's classification, 98
  Multilingual Aphasia Examination, subtest
    of, 102
  pantomime recognition, 63, 68
  phoneme discrimination, 101–4
  three-dimensional block construction, 118–9
Auditory discrimination
  in aphasia, 98
  and phoneme discrimination, 98

Bilateral hemisphere lesions
  digit span, 29
  finger localization, 93–95
  motor impersistence, 133
  right–left orientation, 15–16
  serial digit learning, 28–29
  tactile form perception, 80–82
  temporal orientation, 6
  three-dimensional block construction, block
    models, 118
  visual form discrimination, 59–60
Body schema
  finger localization and, 84
  right–left orientation and, 10
Brainstem injury. *See* Closed head injury

Children, performances of
  facial recognition, 35–36
  finger localization, 89, 92–93, 95–96